THE LIBRARIAN AS
INFORMATION
CONSULTANT

D1567930

DATE DUE

11/12/14	

DEMCO, INC. 38-2931

ALA Editions purchases fund advocacy, awareness, and accreditation programs for library professionals worldwide.

THE LIBRARIAN AS INFORMATION CONSULTANT

Transforming Reference for the Information Age

Sarah Anne Murphy

AMERICAN LIBRARY ASSOCIATION
CHICAGO   2011

Sarah Anne Murphy has held numerous positions at The Ohio State University since 1999. She is currently coordinator of research and reference for the OSU Libraries. Murphy earned a master of business administration from The Ohio State University Fisher College of Business in 2008 and her master of library science from Kent State University in 2000. She has published papers on Lean Six Sigma, mentoring, and issues related to veterinary medicine libraries in *College and Research Libraries,* the *Journal of Academic Librarianship,* and the *Journal of the Medical Library Association.*

© 2011 by the American Library Association

Printed in the United States of America
15 14 13 12 11   5 4 3 2 1

ISBN: 978-0-8389-1086-3

Library of Congress Cataloging-in-Publication Data
Murphy, Sarah Anne.
 The librarian as information consultant : transforming reference for the information age / Sarah Anne Murphy.
    p. cm.
 Includes bibliographical references and index.
 ISBN 978-0-8389-1086-3 (alk. paper)
 1. Reference services (Libraries)—Forecasting. 2. Reference services (Libraries)—Management. 3. Information consultants. 4. Reference librarians—Effect of technological innovations on. I. Title.
 Z711.M87 2011
 025.5'2—dc22
                                                                                    2010043518

Cover design by Chelsea McGorisk. Interior design in Minion Pro and Union by Casey Bayer.

ALA Editions also publishes its books in a variety of electronic formats. For more information, visit the ALA Store at www.alastore.ala.org and select eEditions.

CONTENTS

INTRODUCTION

Why write a book on library and information consulting, or more specifically, on repositioning reference librarians to function as library and information consultants? In January 2008 I accepted a new position at The Ohio State University as coordinator of research and reference. While I intuitively understood my role, I still had many questions. After three years in exile off-campus, the university's main library was preparing to move back to its renovated facility during the summer of 2009, and I was fielding questions from administrators, library faculty, and staff regarding how the reference desk would be staffed when the new building opened. Some pressed whether the desk was still needed, while others adamantly argued it was. This astounded me, as I couldn't reconcile unleashing more than fifty thousand undergraduate students into an eleven-floor, 202,047-square-foot building without defined service points. I started reading the debates in the library literature about the future of the reference desk and quickly realized that many of my colleagues were confusing the desk with their professional value and worth as reference librarians.[1] Just what is a reference librarian anyway? Although the definition for *reference* from the Reference and User Services Association (RUSA) now recognizes the fact that reference is much broader than a single transaction with a consumer, could the reference desk debate really be about the word *reference* itself?[2]

Reference librarians have a strong history of matching information to consumers' information needs. Information, however, is no longer location-dependent in today's networked society, and libraries now have many competitors willing and able to satisfy an individual's information needs (regardless of quality). To remain competitive, reference librarians must focus on their strengths as advisors, helping consumers to understand the structure of information both within and outside of our library facilities, to make sense of the information found, and to use this information in the format (books, e-journals, microform, etc.) presented. As library and information consultants, reference librarians are well-positioned to adapt to shifting consumer expectations and the changing information environment.

The premise of this book is that reference librarians must reposition themselves as library and information consultants. The book is grounded in the fundamentals required for sustaining a successful consulting practice. A small subgroup of librarians already function as information brokers or consultants for both libraries and the public sector, usually providing independent research services. Some function as library consultants exclusively, advising library organizations on issues such as reorganizing departmental staff, the implementation of new products or services, or the reconfiguration of existing library space.[3] Within the library profession, however, the concept of consultant is applied more broadly. A number of library and information science publications include various forms of the word in their titles. Jastram and Zawistoski, for instance, define information consulting as "dedicated uninterrupted time to work collaboratively with a patron."[4] LaBaugh focuses on the historical and current advisory role of reference librarians, noting that like consultants, they function as counselors who help "clients define basic problems and establish strategies for dealing with those problems."[5]

Many articles discuss consulting within the context of library instruction. Cheney uses the term loosely while describing librarians' involvement in the structure and design of coursework using problem-based learning teaching methods.[6] Kraemer and Yi both use the term to describe dedicated one-on-one instruction to assist patrons with developing strategies for locating information for a specific project.[7] Debons et al. and Whitlatch use the concept of knowledge counselors, or individuals ready to diagnose and offer solutions for a consumer's information need, particularly for those questions with no definitive correct answer.[8] Whitlatch in particular notes that for such questions, "Librarians cannot do all the research for all outside inquirers and fax them the results. Readers themselves must still conduct most of the research into records of our civilization within the walls of real libraries."[9]

Perhaps the concept of consulting introduced by Frank et al. relates most to the chapters and reasoning of the author of this book.[10] Arguing that librarians must become effective consultants to remain relevant on their campuses, Frank and his colleagues advocate proactive engagement with faculty and students on campus through the provision of value-added services supported by client-centered marketing campaigns. This requires "understanding the client's needs, shaping solutions around a client's actual needs rather than what the consultant thinks the client requires, and communicating clearly with clients . . . in the academic setting."[11]

Reference librarians must embrace their role as library and information consultants, by first recognizing their traditional advisory role for matching consumers' information needs with the resources available to satisfy those needs, and then adapting the business model and practices of consultants working outside of the library and information science profession. In an information environment crowded with distractions and competitors for library consumers' attention, librarians must reposition themselves to maintain their effectiveness, visibility, and value to the clients they serve.

The terms client, consumer, and customer rather than library patron or user are deliberately used throughout this book. The author prefers these terms, especially because the word *user*, when unqualified, has acquired negative connotations in the North American vernacular. Most industries refer to the individuals who purchase their goods and services as consumers or customers. The author believes the library community would benefit from using these terms, which are universally understood both within and outside of library organizations. Further, by referring to our library patron groups as consumers or customers, we are recognizing that individuals choose to use a library's resources and services, just as they choose to use another information commodity, such as a bookstore or website, to seek an answer to their questions or information to resolve their problems.

To reposition librarians as library and information consultants, each chapter of this book introduces many tools and concepts covered during the course of a traditional MBA program. Chapter 1 focuses on defining consulting and why it is important for libraries and reference librarians in particular. It addresses some myths and concerns librarians have for adopting business practices and frames the potential utility for library and information consultants in the Google Age. It also discusses the skills and characteristics of successful consultants that can be applied to library practice.

Chapter 2 addresses the most significant discipline for a consultant practice: building and maintaining client relationships. Consultants understand they will have no business if they have no clients. This means they devote a significant amount of time, energy, and resources to develop and maintain a client base. This chapter introduces factors to consider when designing or redesigning a service process. The Voice of the Customer concept is introduced with a discussion centered on its importance and its value for designing and maintaining quality services. Because service failure will occur regardless of how well a service process is designed, the concept of service recovery is also covered, encouraging library and information consultants to build plans for service recovery into their service processes.

Chapter 3 introduces services marketing, focusing on the tools and concepts required to cultivate the library and information consultant's brand identity and the brand identity of service products in general. The value of both developing and understanding a ServiceScape is discussed, as the environment in which a customer uses a service influences his opinion of that service. The service blueprint is introduced as a valuable tool for detailing and visualizing the service process. Advice is then provided for developing and implementing a marketing plan and an integrated marketing communications strategy.

Chapter 4 focuses on managing employee service roles and customer demand. The Integrated Gaps Model of Service Quality is introduced to provide a framework to discuss the activities required and skills needed to close the gaps between customer expectations and the actual service provided. Employee roles in the delivery of library and information consulting services are detailed. The chapter discusses managing fluctuations in customer demand with consultant supply and concludes by offering a brief introduction to managing financial and capital resources using impact evaluation.

Chapter 5 begins by examining the costs of quality, and then provides an overview of three quality improvement frameworks or disciplines that provide an infrastructure for ensuring the library and information consultant is delivering the service promised to their customers: Lean, Six Sigma, and the Baldrige National Quality Program. Each has a demonstrated utility for improving customer service and fostering a learning organization.

Armed with an understanding of the tools and concepts driving consultants' model of practice, reference librarians may better engage library consumers by assuming their role as library and information consultants.

Notes

1. Sarah Barbara Watstein and Steven J. Bell, "Is There a Future for the Reference Desk? A Point–Counterpoint Discussion," *Reference Librarian* 49, no. 1 (January 2008): 1–20.
2. American Library Association, "Reference and User Services Association, Definitions of Reference," www.ala.org/ala/mgrps/divs/rusa/resources/guidelines/definitionsreference.cfm.
3. Ulla De Stricker, *Is Consulting for You? A Primer for Information Professionals* (Chicago: American Library Association, 2008).
4. Iris Jastram and Ann Zawistoski, "Personalizing the Library via Research Consultations," in *The Desk and Beyond: Next Generation Reference Services,* ed. Sarah K. Steiner and M. Leslie Madden (Chicago: Association of College and Research Libraries, 2008), 14–24.
5. Ross T. LaBaugh, "Solution Focused Reference: Counselor Librarianship Revisited," in *The Desk and Beyond: Next Generation Reference Services,* ed. Sarah K. Steiner and M. Leslie Madden (Chicago: Association of College and Research Libraries, 2008), 38–52.
6. Debora Cheney, "Problem-Based Learning: Librarians as Collaborators and Consultants," *portal: Libraries and the Academy* 4, no. 4 (October 2004): 495–508.
7. Elizabeth W. Kraemer, "Developing Information Literacy Instruction for Honors Students at Oakland University: An Information Consulting Approach," *College and Undergraduate Libraries* 14, no. 3 (September 2007): 63–73; Hua Yi, "Individual Research Consultation Service: An Important Part of an Information Literacy Program," *Reference Services Review* 31, no. 4 (2003): 342–50.
8. Anthony Debons, et al., "Knowledge Counseling: The Concept, the Process, and Its Application," in *Knowledge Management for the Information Professional,* ed. T. Kanti Srikantaiah and Michael E. D. Koenig (Medford, NJ: American Society for Information Science by Information Today, 2000), 459–79; Jo Bell Whitlatch, "Reference Futures: Outsourcing, the Web, Or Knowledge Counseling," *Reference Services Review* 31, no. 1 (2003): 26–30.
9. Ibid., 27.
10. Donald G. Frank, Gregory K. Raschke, Julie Wood, and Julie Z. Yang, "Information Consulting: The Key to Success in Academic Libraries," *Journal of Academic Librarianship* 27, no. 2 (March 2001): 90–98.
11. Ibid., 94.

1

The Library and Information Consultant

Almost every management book on consulting starts with a definition of consulting and states how you can profit by marketing your skills and advice to others. But like librarianship, consulting as a profession is ill-defined. While physicians must graduate from medical school, spend years in internships and residencies, and maintain licensure to practice, consultants have no such requirements. Yet numerous for-profit and not-for-profit firms hire consultants to facilitate change, acquire knowledge, or influence others. Businesses recognize consultants' value because consultants consistently deliver results while communicating their value to the constituents they serve. This discipline is imperative for consultants' survival, and librarians can learn from their example.

This chapter focuses on defining consulting and identifying the similarities and parallels that currently exist between successful consultants and successful reference librarians. It argues that reference librarians in essence are already functioning as consultants, sharing their expertise surrounding the structure and function of information and the library organization itself. It presents the reasons why a consumer may be interested in using a library and information consultant's services while discussing her value in the Age of Google. It follows by identifying the talents and characteristics of successful consultants, which also apply to a successful library and information consultant. It concludes with a discussion of the myths and realities surrounding the adoption of business practices in libraries and other nonprofit organizations to show that repositioning reference librarians as library and information consultants will not detract from the library profession itself.

Consulting Defined

Few individuals outside of the library profession truly understand a reference librarian's skills or appreciate the years of education and work experience required to become an effective, proficient purveyor of information. While one *Oxford English Dictionary* definition for a consultant begins with "a person qualified to give professional advice or services," it ends with "a private detective." Another definition in the same dictionary entry refers to a consultant as "(an oracle)." Any reference librarian, whether in a public or academic library setting, functions both as a private detective and an oracle, yet these terms are not used to describe her work or profession.

Consultants focus on results, helping clients to define their needs, acquire the competencies and skills to address these needs, and take action. In the process, the consultant leads the client from a state of unconscious incompetency to unconscious competency.[1] As advisors, consultants rely on the information and knowledge they've acquired over their careers to identify solutions and guide their employers in implementing them. They have many roles. Some are hired for their knowledge of and experience with a particular product or process, such as retail design consultants, who focus on helping stores maximize aesthetics and layout to stimulate sales. Others are hired for their ability to affect change, helping an organization to realize its strategic plan, or successfully redesign services following the implementation of new technology.

Parallels between the Competencies of Successful Consultants and the Competencies of Successful Reference Librarians

Table 1.1 outlines the competencies of a successful consultant that parallel those of a successful reference librarian, as defined by the American Library Association's "Guidelines for the Behavioral Performance of Reference and Information Service Providers."[2] Like librarians, consultants must have the ability to actively listen to a client's information need and translate that need into a workable solution. Consultants spend considerable time assisting clients with defining their problem, just as reference librarians assist consumers with developing their information query. Consultants interview their clients to clarify the problem discussed, using open and closed questions and other techniques to determine the scope and parameters of their assignment. In some instances, the client may be well aware that something is wrong, but unable to define what that something is. The consultant may assist the client by paraphrasing what he has heard so far, using the client's own words. The consultant may also seek raw data, investigate industry trends, or interview individual company employees to reach a shared definition for the problem.

Reference librarians also interview consumers with information needs to clarify terminology, seek additional information that is relevant to their

---

Table 1.1

Parallel Competencies of Successful Consultants and Successful Reference Librarians

COMPETENCIES OF SUCCESSFUL CONSULTANTS	COMPETENCIES OF SUCCESSFUL REFERENCE LIBRARIANS
Listening ■ actively hears and clarifies client's needs, as stated in client's own words Investigative ■ systematically seeks data or information Analytical ■ examines the data collected to identify sources of variation, solutions, and/or opportunities for improvement Action ■ implements solutions ■ manages change	Approachability ■ welcomes patron with verbal and nonverbal behaviors that put patron at ease ■ provides assistance at patron's point of need Interest ■ confirms understanding of patron's information needs Listening/Inquiring ■ allows patron to state information need in own words ■ rephrases or clarifies patron request Searching ■ formulates an effective search strategy with patron Follow-up ■ asks patron if her question was answered ■ encourages patron to return for assistance

research, understand the overarching objective or goal driving the consumer's research, and discover what information the consumer has already located to avoid duplicate effort. While the consultant will formulate and execute a data collection plan to research the client's problem, the reference librarian will work with the consumer to construct a search strategy. The consultant will seek to identify the root cause of his client's problem. The librarian will look for information in a format desired by the consumer that has the potential to satisfy the consumer's information need. Both the consultant and librarian will adjust their activities to reflect the depth of detail desired by the client or consumer. This means the reference librarian will limit her search to peer-reviewed articles if she's assisting a researcher applying for a scientific grant, or images for an artist designing a community mural. The consultant may conduct a complex statistical analysis but repackage the results in a narrative with executive summary.

The consultant will apply his expertise while investigating the client's problem, and the reference librarian will apply hers during the search. The reference librarian's expertise lies in her understanding of the structure and function of information and her broad knowledge of sources to guide the consumer's search. In large public libraries, she may be assigned to a specific subject area, such as business, social sciences, or readers' advisory. In academic settings, a general reference librarian may specialize in one or more subjects. To answer a patron's question, she may need to collaborate with a local library colleague with understanding of a foreign language or culture, or a librarian in another country to provide assistance to the consumer.

Following the interviews and collection of data, the librarian and the consultant each work to make sense of the information gathered. The consultant will attempt to identify discrepancies between the client's desired outcomes and actual outcomes using statistics and other analytical tools as required. He will seek the root cause of the client's problem in an effort to formulate recommendations for improvement. The consultant will then brainstorm, prioritize, and review all possible solutions to identify those that will best address the problem. The librarian will work with the consumer to evaluate the results of the search, the quality and quantity of information retrieved, and whether the information answered the consumer's question or satisfied his need. The librarian will encourage the consumer to approach her again if he has additional questions, or if the initial information discovered did not result in a workable solution to his problem.

Throughout all stages of the process, the librarian will be pushing the consumer to refine his information need as presented. Additional information may be required to clarify the consumer's information need and improve the recall or specificity of the search. The librarian may encourage the consumer to consider the scope of his query more broadly or focus his search using specific keywords. The consultant will be engaged in similar work, pushing his client to refine the scope of the project and his objectives for conducting the investigation. Such questioning continues as the investigative and analytical stages of the consultation process, until a workable solution is achieved or the desired information is located.

Why Hire a Consultant?
The Value of the Library and Information Consultant in the Age of Google

Why should a reference librarian function as a library and information consultant? Consumers have a financial incentive to act on a consultant's advice. In purchasing a consultant's services, they have invested a considerable amount of time, staff resources, and money. They expect the advice they receive will be of value and result in a measurable return on their investment. Consumers also invest in library services when seeking an answer to a question. Although their incentives for seeking advice may differ, their motivations usually involve saving time, minimizing frustration, and maximizing understanding. This is especially true in the Age of Google, where tidbits of information can be retrieved at any time, in any location.

It is of interest to examine librarians' value to consumers by evaluating the strengths, weaknesses, and opportunities of the profession, and the library as a cultural entity itself. This is especially true as libraries struggle to adapt in an era of rapid, transformative change. As Google, eBay, Craigslist, and other services have revealed the Internet's remarkable potential for serving the diverse interests of the general public, such an evaluation may enlighten, inform, and provide the impetus for reference librarians to perceive themselves differently. Demand for library materials in this environment, for example, has transformed, as services such as Google Books have demonstrated their utility by serving both broad and niche interest groups. Web 2.0 technologies have also demonstrated their utility, enabling individuals to maintain contact with family and friends and interact with a broader realm of individuals holding similar interests, regardless of whether they live in distant cities or countries.

But although technology reveals exciting opportunities, it doesn't replace human interaction. Yes, the Internet has fundamentally changed reference librarians' work; it hasn't supplanted their value. Today if a consumer needs to translate a sentence from an unfamiliar language to English, he will use Babelfish or another freely available translation website, rather than locate a library's bilingual dictionaries. Further, why should a consumer visit the library to use a directory when phone numbers and addresses for organizations are freely available online? If a consumer needs to know the amount of soybeans produced by Ohio farmers during the last year, he'll seek this fact himself, as statistics which were once only found in libraries' print government documents collections are now almost exclusively online. As long as the consumer can verify the authenticity and quality of the information located, the Internet is a remarkable tool for straightforward, time-sensitive, factually driven information.

But librarians understand the Internet can also seductively entice a consumer to remain trapped in a void of miscellaneous blurbs, some correct, some incorrect. With everyone as a potential author, consumers must learn to utilize the information found online with caution, and resist the temptation to rely on immediate, instantly gratifying text which can be purposefully misleading or grossly out of context. Many consumers haven't acquired this skill, getting frustrated, terrified, and confused when their serendipitous online wandering fails to satisfy their needs. They realize the Internet is a huge amoeba and find their way back to libraries, seeking the in-depth information that library collections provide. This is particularly true when consumers need to learn a new skill or understand a complex issue.[3] The in-depth collections libraries construct are a strength, along with libraries' ability to organize information.

Still, many of us take our access to the Internet for granted, failing to remember some of our neighbors lack the financial resources to purchase a computer and support monthly connectivity charges. Libraries bridge the technology gap and much more. As a cultural institution, libraries were "created *to hold* and preserve objects and texts, *to expand* the boundaries of public knowledge associated with those artifacts and words, and *to open* the possibilities of learning in the contexts of everyday life."[4] Learning is a social activity and libraries, museums, zoological gardens, and parks all work to inform their constituencies and stimulate personal reflection. Libraries provide an environment where consumers can slow down, locate information either in a physical or digital form, and assimilate it with their own ideas and values. Libraries contribute to a community's social capital, generating wealth and value by supporting consumers' need for personal and professional growth, providing referral to community agencies and organizations, empowering consumers to make informed decisions, supporting cultural awareness and diversity, and making spaces available for individuals to meet.

Google cannot and will not replace library services. Yes, consumers can obtain some factual information on their own, without library mediation. The sheer amount of information retrieved via Internet searches, however, often intimidates, rather than empowers the consumer. The reference librarian who both functions as and promotes herself as a library and information consultant is better positioned to communicate her skills as an experienced expert who can seamlessly navigate both the Internet and the library, saving the consumer time and energy by matching him with the desired information regardless of format. Funding instead may be the library's greatest threat for future survival, as funding enables libraries to sustain the innovative services and programs, collections, and facilities that consumers value. In such an environment, libraries must become more consumer-focused, defining customer needs in customer terms to develop and customize services and market new and existing products. An additional challenge is overcoming our preference for forcing consumers to seek our assistance only after exhausting Internet search options. As noted by Michael Baldwin, "We must stop being enablers for garbage information and become tough-love interveners with real information." In this role, "We need to see our jobs as actually informing people rather than as simply making information available."[5]

Talents and Characteristics of a Successful Consultant

As "tough-love interveners" the ideal library and information consultant should share some of the talents and characteristics that contribute to a consultant's success. Such traits go beyond professional competencies which can be acquired through training and experience, and include

> in-depth knowledge of industry or expertise in a specific skill or
>   management technique
> appreciation for risk
> self-confidence
> self-mastery
> ability to work hard
> comfort communicating with individuals in a variety of settings
>   and levels within an organization
> ability to self-promote and prospect clients
> self-discipline
> ability to empower client(s) and understand client as a problem-
>   solving partner
> flexibility/adaptability
> facilitation/motivation skills
> leadership skills
> detail orientation
> tolerance for routine
> analytical skills
> honesty/integrity
> objectivity
> accountability for actions and results

Most notably, like librarians, whose expertise lies in the organization of information and libraries, consultants usually have an in-depth knowledge of a particular industry, such as oil or health care, or a competency in a specific discipline such as Lean Six Sigma or database design. Beyond expertise, however, the consulting profession tends to attract individuals who appreciate risk, possess self-confidence and mastery, are willing to work hard to achieve success, and are able to take a broad view of an industry or organization. Successful consultants are comfortable speaking with individuals in a variety of settings and levels within an organization, communicate well with others, and enjoy selling themselves. They remain aware of both their personal limitations and their limitations in knowledge so that they may reject projects beyond their ability to assist or outside the scope of their business strategy and refer those projects to others. Successful consultants exercise extreme self-discipline and hold themselves accountable for remaining current in their area of expertise. They understand this is crucial because their livelihood depends on their knowledge. Those who have mastered their craft shift from functioning as "a savior and problem-solver to being an empowering partner."[6] Such a skill is necessary to reach a mutual understanding of the client's problem and identify a workable solution.

To succeed as a consultant, one must learn to prospect clients in addition to selling oneself. Further, one has to remain flexible to adapt to the client's environment, seek multiple and creative solutions to the clients' identified problem, and motivate both oneself and the client to create change and implement solutions which address the root cause of the problem. Consultants must be skilled with facilitating meetings and training others. In some instances they are hired to facilitate conflict resolution for a group; in others, to teach a team a new skill. Consultants must possess leadership skills and have the ability to wear multiple hats. With an entrepreneurial mindset, they understand a positive attitude is required to weather the challenges presented. Frustration may be inevitable, but can be managed. The successful consultant must believe that he can influence results. Further, he must use his knowledge of the industry or organization, and have the ability to identify valuable relationships that may have previously been discounted or overlooked. Orientation to detail and a tolerance for routine tasks are also required to effectively analyze collected data and project results.

Successful consultants possess integrity and are both willing and able to dispense the honest truth to their clients, even if telling the truth risks their dismissal and subsequent loss of income. They confront problems directly, often providing a client or organization much-needed objectivity. They develop a network of colleagues to both consult and refer clients to when appropriate. The successful consultant also demonstrates a certain resourcefulness for locating the tools and expertise needed to get the job done. Like librarians, he protects his clients' right to privacy or confidentiality. Although consultants aren't required to subscribe to the Association of Professional Consultant's "Code of Ethics," successful consultants adhere to similar standards.[7] They are accountable for their actions or inactions, understanding that they affect results. Humble, consultants are able to say,

"I don't know" when appropriate, and either work with the client to figure out the issue or refer the client to someone with the appropriate expertise. Honest, they refuse to promise more than they can deliver. Successful consultants also ask satisfied clients for referrals. This proactive marketing technique is a simple way to identify new clients and make them aware of the services you offer.

Many successful reference librarians already exhibit the talents and characteristics of successful consultants. Given the freedom to reconceptualize their library skills and background, they can function as consultants if they are not doing so already. By marketing ourselves as library and information consultants, librarians have a greater opportunity to showcase the talents our communities rely on, using a language and discipline to which our communities can relate.

Why Adopt Business Practices in Libraries and Other Nonprofit Organizations

It is true that libraries are not a business and cannot function exclusively like one. Like a great business, however, a well-managed, respected library requires disciplined planning, personnel, governance, and allocation of resources to succeed.[8] Libraries can successfully adapt a number of business principles, tools, and concepts to learn about their organizations and forward their missions. The way consultants conceptualize, organize, and market their practices offers much utility to librarians, if librarians are receptive to considering themselves and their profession differently. This requires setting aside preconceptions about the traditional role of the librarian and the activities that contribute to the success of a library's reference service.

Nonprofits in general have a tendency to attract individuals who are passionate about their organization's mission and the services it provides. The library profession is no exception. Individuals are attracted to professional librarianship for a variety of reasons. Some value free access to information and understand its importance for a democratic society. Others may be passionate readers or enjoy the thrill of tracking down an elusive answer to a patron's question. Some love the public institution of the library, while others are attracted to public service in general. Regardless of the reasoning driving a librarian's decision to enter the profession, it is dangerous for anyone to fail to appreciate and recognize that libraries have a business component, which must be managed effectively. Adopting business practices to the operation and delivery of library services is not necessarily evil or out of sync with a library's mission. Further, skill in marketing, operations, training, education, and management is necessary for a library or library service operation to thrive and succeed.

Pamela Wilcox highlights the many myths and misconceptions circulating among staff and the public regarding libraries and other nonprofit organizations in her book *Exposing the Elephants: Creating Exceptional Nonprofits*. She notes a number of myths, including the idea that nonprofits exist only to further the public good.[9] Like the for-profit sector, financial resources are required to advance the nonprofit's mission. Unlike the commercial sector, however, profit resulting from revenue minus costs is expressed in different terms. Money does not equate success in the library and nonprofit sectors, but rather influences the outcomes of the financial investment in relation to the organization's mission. Reliant on the communities they serve for financial resources, and on friends, donors, and grant-making agencies to supplement these resources, libraries must be good stewards of the resources bestowed upon them by spending their funds in the most efficient and effective manner possible.

It is also a myth that success cannot be measured quantitatively in the library and nonprofit sector. Although it is true that libraries are extremely proficient at counting outputs such as the number of circulation transactions, the number of individuals served at a reference desk, the number of books in their collections, or the number of instructional sessions given, the plethora of library assessment conferences and publications in recent years indicates that libraries and librarians still struggle with measuring and communicating outcomes.[10] Libraries, and reference librarians in particular, must master this skill, especially because they are competing for the limited resources both within their organization and with others seeking financial support within their communities. Governments, universities, granting organizations, donors, and other providers of financial resources will invest funds elsewhere if they do not see a demonstrated return on their investment. Therefore libraries cannot afford to waste their productivity, talent, and time on ineffective services and programs.

Perhaps the largest myth, however, is the idea that libraries and other nonprofit sector organizations already operate well, especially considering staffing and funding resource limitations, the conflicts between professional managers and volunteer boards, mission creep, and other factors.[11] Wilcox argues that many nonprofit organizations get trapped in a pattern of calm and crisis, resulting from failure to develop and implement a long-term strategy for success.

The reality is that great libraries and nonprofit organizations have much in common with great businesses.[12] They are able to deliver superior performance year after year, with more complex governance systems, financial constraints, staffing limitations, and other factors than their for-profit brethren. With discipline, focus, and a strategy for sustained results, libraries and other nonprofit organizations can and do achieve greatness, advancing their mission for the constituents they serve. Libraries and librarians cannot shy away from business principles and practices, sheltering themselves by relying on research and lessons learned within the library sector itself. There is much to be learned by observing and adapting competencies and tools of other professionals, particularly those in the consulting profession.

Summary

Reference librarians already share a number of competencies and talents with successful consultants. By appreciating these similarities and capitalizing on the differences, reference librarians may strengthen their ability to communicate their value by repositioning themselves as library and information consultants. By approaching reference work from the perspective of a consultant, librarians can better help consumers to recognize the value the reference librarian brings to their quest for information.

The reference librarian's role has transformed in the Age of Google. The Internet cannot and will not replace human interaction. Consumers will continue to seek libraries and the individuals who work within them for reasoned advice on locating quality information both efficiently and effectively. The library and information consultant must proactively seek clients, rather than focusing almost exclusively on making information available in case it is needed in the future. Because great libraries have much in common with great businesses, there should be no apprehension with repositioning reference librarians as library and information consultants. With strategic competitive planning, along with the disciplined allocation of financial, human, and capital resources, a great library will deliver superior performance that is reflected by measured outcomes, year after year. By thinking and acting as library and information consultants, reference librarians will be better positioned to deliver superior results to the communities they serve.

Notes

1. Alan Weiss, *Million Dollar Consulting: The Professional's Guide to Growing a Practice* (New York: McGraw-Hill, 2003).
2. American Library Association, Reference and User Services Association, "Guidelines for the Behavioral Performance of Reference and Information Service Providers," www.ala.org/Template.cfm?Section=Home&template=/ContentManagement/ContentDisplay.cfm&ContentID=26937.
3. Larry Keller, "Not an Endangered Career: Looking It Up," CNN.com, November 28, 2000. http://archives.cnn.com/2000/CAREER/trends/11/28/librarians.
4. David Carr, *The Promise of Cultural Institutions* (Walnut Creek, CA: AltaMira Press, 2003), xii.
5. Michael Baldwin, "Librarians as Knowledge Provocateurs," *Public Libraries* 45, no. 2 (2006): 11–14.
6. Keith Merron, *Consulting Mastery: How the Best Make the Biggest Difference* (San Francisco: Berrett-Koehler Publishers, 2005).
7. Association of Professional Consultants, "Code of Ethics," www.consultapc.org/files/codeofethics.doc.
8. James C. Collins, *Good to Great and the Social Sectors: Why Business Thinking Is Not the Answer: A Monograph to Accompany Good to Great: Why Some Companies Make the Leap—and Others Don't* (Boulder, CO: J. Collins, 2005).
9. Pamela J. Wilcox, *Exposing the Elephants: Creating Exceptional Nonprofits* (Hoboken, NJ: John Wiley and Sons, 2006).
10. Association of Research Libraries, "Library Assessment Conference: Building Effective, Sustainable, Effective Practice," http://libraryassessment.org.
11. *Exposing the Elephants.*
12. *Good to Great.*

2

Strategies for Building and Maintaining Consumer Relationships

The Voice of the Customer

Because this book argues that reference librarians must reposition themselves as library and information consultants to successfully serve their constituent populations, the remaining chapters focus on the tools and mindset required for librarians to transition to the library and information consultant role. First and foremost, any good consultant recognizes that for her business to succeed, she must have clients. Thus consultants take a disciplined approach to finding and maintaining client relationships. This requires that they know their market and understand the difference between publicity and public relations. Consultants must understand and accept that in many instances their ability to prospect new clients is challenged, as clients are often unaware they could benefit from a consultant's services. Because of clients' lack of knowledge, consultants must become both comfortable and proficient with making cold calls, developing and maintaining newsletters and blogs, and seizing public speaking opportunities. Marketing skills and a marketing plan are imperative. Service quality is also critical as satisfied clients attract new clients, through referral, word of mouth, or viral marketing.

This chapter will focus on developing the Voice of the Customer, the backbone of any service operation and marketing plan, and translating this voice into the technical requirements that satisfy consumers' needs. Since most consultants operate independently, the chapter begins with an overview of service industries in general and service process design to illustrate how the library and information consultant fits within the context of library operations. It continues by defining the Voice of the Customer, exploring methods to obtain this information and describing the steps to take to both elicit consumer requirements and develop or redevelop new or existing services. The chapter concludes with a discussion centered on the most important aspect of managing service experiences: service recovery.

Introduction to Service Process Design: Factors to Consider

As the United States transforms into a service economy, more and more individuals are working in the services sector. Services differ significantly from manufactured goods, as the service product is both intangible and heterogeneous.[1] Management of the service product is especially challenging, as services are produced and consumed simultaneously by the service provider and consumer. This means a service cannot be stored or transported. Fluctuations in customer demand require employers to design efficient and effective staff schedules to meet this demand. Further, the high degree of consumer interaction necessary for successful delivery of some services affects service providers' efficiency and ability to deliver a quality product.

A service provider must define the service product if he wishes to optimally design a service process. Considering the intangible quality of services, this may be particularly challenging. Most services come bundled in a package, which consists of three elements:

- the *facilitating goods,* represented by the physical goods purchased;
- the *explicit, or tangible, service* provided;
- and the *implicit service,* as evidenced by the psychological service the consumer experiences.[2]

Thus, if you visit an amusement park, the rides themselves represent the facilitating goods. You purchased access to the Magnum XL-200 roller coaster with your admissions ticket. The various themes, smells, and food at Storybook Land, along with the cleanliness of restrooms and the friendliness and approachability of staff, represent the tangible service. The psychological service is evidenced by the fun you have with your family and friends while at the park.

An understanding of the service-product bundle offered by a library organization is necessary for any library and information consultant to have a foundation for designing and promoting the library's consulting services.

With the right mix of facilitating goods, tangible services, and psychological services, the library and the library and information consultant will meet customer expectations. Overall, the library building itself represents a facilitating good in most library organizations, along with the library's computers and physical collection. This has increasingly been recognized in recent years as a critical element for encouraging and maintaining consumers' use of library facilities and library-consumer relationships.[3] Design does matter. Thus an academic library must provide spaces for group study and quiet contemplation. A public library may consider updating its children's area to meet the needs of both parents and its younger constituents. Further, in the online environment, the library's website is also a facilitating good, regardless of whether it is used within or outside of the library's physical walls. This site is often the only portal used by a number of library constituents seeking to access the vast electronic collections and services provided by the library.

Tangible library services are represented by such elements as cleanliness or friendly, available, and helpful staff. These elements can be measured using checklists, focus groups, or customer satisfaction surveys. The psychological service provided by the library is evidenced by the delight of an undergraduate student who realizes a library offers a distraction-free place to study, or by the newfound confidence a financially struggling father displays after receiving assistance from a librarian when seeking employment. Indeed, anthropologists recognize librarians as keystone species, noting that communities suffer when library services and organizations are overlooked.[4]

In addition to the service-product bundle, the library and information consultant must also consider the degree of consumer interaction and customization required for each service, as this has a profound impact on the service's efficiency as well as the human and capital resources required for effective delivery. Library services such as interlibrary loan and circulation can effectively serve customers with a high degree of automation. The library and information consultant's services will likely require a high degree of customer interaction and product customization, heightening labor intensity. Navigating a library, for instance, can be relatively straightforward if the consumer knows the specific author or title of the book he is looking for. Information seeking becomes more nebulous when a consumer doesn't know how to start her search or even where to start looking. Thus the library and information consultant must seriously consider available human resources and personnel issues when designing or redesigning library and information consulting services.

Understanding the degree of customer interaction and customization and the service-product bundle is especially important as consumers continually exercise their right to choose. If a service does not meet their expectations, consumers can and will find an alternative to an organization's service product.[5] Their decisions are influenced by a number of factors, including convenience or the overall customer experience.[6] For instance, if a customer finds a local alternative to an organization that provides comparable service, he will switch to the competitor. Further, if an organization requires customers to wait for a service that is readily available from the closest competitor, the organization will lose customers. Employees who exhibit dismissive, impolite, or unresponsive behavior encourage consumers to find other venues in which to conduct their business. Sloppy work, poor response to service failure, ethical transgressions, and pricing also influence consumers' decisions. Thus, an understanding of consumers' reasons for trying or using a competitor's services, in addition to an organization's service-product bundle and the degree of customer interaction required to successfully deliver a service, is required to both design future services and retain current clients.

In all, factors to consider when designing or redesigning a service process include the location of the service, the layout of the location in which the service is provided, product or process design, scheduling, worker skills, quality control and measures, time standards, demand and capacity planning, technology requirements, whether or not to standardize the service offering, the degree of customer contact and interaction, the amount of discretion frontline personnel can have with customers, whether or not it is appropriate to market other library services simultaneously, and customer participation.[7] Table 2.1 offers an example of the design factors to consider when planning service for a circulation desk versus an interlibrary loan office. Note the differences that exist between a traditionally more front-office operation, such as circulation, where employees must interact directly with the public in real time, and an operation such as interlibrary loan, where the bulk of the work is conducted outside of the consumer's view. The varying degrees of customer contact and interaction required of front-office versus back-office operations all affect the quality and design of a service process.

Table 2.1

Service Decision Factors:
Circulation Versus Interlibrary Loan

DESIGN FACTOR	CIRCULATION	INTERLIBRARY LOAN
Facility location	Close to library entrances; visible online presence on library website and in library's electronic resources.	Separate office or co-located with another library function, such as Circulation; visible online presence on library website and in library's electronic resources.
Facility layout	Facility reflects customers' needs for various types of library space (e.g., individual versus group study, story time).	Separate office primarily designed for back-office tasks, such as borrowing, lending, receiving, and processing interlibrary loan requests using software such as OCLC's ILLIAD.
Product and process design	Service focuses on customer access to library materials: includes borrowing, selecting, and retrieving requested material, and the return and reshelving of materials so that other customers may access.	Service enables customers to borrow materials not owned by their library from another library organization.
Scheduling	Employees are scheduled to meet peak customer demand.	Employees are scheduled to satisfy daily requirements of interlibrary loan office.
Worker skills	People skills required, along with understanding of library policies and layout.	Task-orientation required, along with computer skills.
Quality control, measures, time standards	Subjective nature of customized services makes measurement more challenging in some instances. Automation makes other circulation functions relatively easy to observe and measure for quality control.	Easy to quantify number of interlibrary loan transactions, turnaround time, etc.
Demand/ capacity planning	Capacity must meet customer demand on an hourly basis.	Academic libraries must plan capacity to meet demand on a seasonal basis. Other libraries may plan capacity to meet demand on a weekly basis.

cont.

Table 2.1 (cont.)

DESIGN FACTOR	CIRCULATION	INTERLIBRARY LOAN
Technology requirements	Automation can replace some workers. Self-checkout kiosks enable customers to check out their own books. Customers can access their library account online without employee assistance.	Automation can eliminate the need for interlibrary loan staff to rekey and manually track consumer's interlibrary loan requests, reducing errors. Automation also enables consumers to track the status of their requests online, enhancing service.
Standardization	Operating policies standardized across a library system. Customer interaction unique to each location.	Interlibrary loan software is standardized across library systems. Thus if a consumer is accustomed to using a product such as OCLC's ILLIAD at one institution, he will be familiar with the ILLIAD interface at another institution.
Customer contact/ interaction	High	Low
Discretion of frontline personnel	High, within the confines of library policy.	Low. Must adhere to federal copyright guidelines.
Marketing	Greater opportunity to promote other library programs and services.	Limited opportunity to promote other library programs and services.
Customer participation	Hybrid of self-service and employee-assisted service.	Mostly self-service. Customer submits request and interlibrary loan office processes behind the scenes.

Designing a Service Process to Reflect the Voice of the Customer

The term *Voice of the Customer* is used by the business and product development community to define the process for identifying "the stated and unstated needs or requirements of the customer."[8] Systematically gathering Voice of the Customer data can dramatically help an organization to identify and translate consumer requirements into the necessary technical requirements to provide consumers with the highest quality service product or offering. (See figure 2.1.) The process encompasses gathering, sorting, developing, and translating customer needs into satisfying products and services. When used in concert with the considerations listed above, identifying the Voice of the Customer can assist library and information consultants with both developing and sustaining customer relationships.

Service providers often focus on the attributes of a service while failing to consider the consumer's consequences for using the service. This is problematic, especially because consumers base their decisions on whether to use your service on how the service subjectively affects their lives. Thus it is extremely important for a service provider to understand the difference between the attributes and consequences of a service offering.[9] Table 2.2 outlines the differences between an attribute and a consequence. Generally attributes are objective, measurable characteristics of a service and may be physical or abstract. Consequences, in contrast, represent the results of using a service. This involves the consumer's perceptions of the service, which is much more difficult to measure. In a library setting for example, accuracy may be considered an attribute of cataloging. With accurate cataloging, a consumer may be able to find what she is looking for within a few minutes, helping her to gather the materials that she needs quickly so that she can move on to her next class assignment. Table 2.3 illustrates other attributes and consequences for select library services. Note that most services have more than one attribute, and that an attribute may have additional consequences for a consumer.

Consultants must have an adequate understanding of their service's attributes and consequences when prospecting new clients. They gain this

Figure 2.1

The Voice of the Customer Process

GATHER ⟹ SORT ⟹ DEVELOP ⟹ TRANSLATE

• Active and Passive Information
• Affinity Diagram
• Card Sorts
• CTQC Tree
• Quality Function Deployment

understanding by actively gathering information through networking, interviewing potential clients, and collecting and analyzing data on the communities they serve. Such activity is necessary, particularly as consequences are subjective and specific to the individual. But consequences themselves are difficult to elicit from consumers. Often consumers are unable to recognize or verbalize consequences that influence their decisions. Furthermore, consequences are continually shifting. The Kano model can explain this phenomenon. Developed by Professor Noriaki Kano in the 1980s, the Kano model (figure 2.2) pictorially displays the consequences driving consumer satisfaction versus an attribute's ability to meet these consequences. Based on the premise that customer loyalty increases with customer satisfaction, Kano defines basic consequences as those the consumer expects of all service brands in a related category. Note the nonlinear relationship between basic consequences and customer satisfaction or loyalty. In the library community, this includes clean public spaces and working computers. Consumers tend to not think about basic consequences, but take them for granted. When an organization fails to deliver on a basic consequence, however, the consumer is extremely dissatisfied.

Attributes Versus Consequences

Table 2.2

ATTRIBUTES	CONSEQUENCES
Attributes are physical or abstract characteristics of the service.	Consequences are a result of using the service.
Attributes are objective.	Consequences are subjective.
Attributes are measurable.	Consequences are measured through surveys of users' perceptions.
Attributes are from the producer's viewpoint.	Consequences are from the consumer's viewpoint.

Source: Caroline Fisher and James T. Schutta, *Developing New Services: Incorporating the Voice of the Customer into Strategic Service Development* (Milwaukee, WI: ASQ Quality Press, 2003) 19.

A direct linear relationship exists for performance consequences, or those consequences consumers currently use to differentiate your brand from another. For instance, a consumer may choose to spend a little more to have her car's oil changed at the garage around the corner from her home because it provides the same service as a discount oil change franchise. Further, this means she's not required to drive across town and then wait two hours for service. Such performance consequences in a library may include timely, accurate answers to patron questions or the availability of a book to check out at the time it is desired.

Excitement consequences are those consequences that are not provided by any other service provider. These represent another nonlinear relationship. When excitement consequences are present, consumer satisfaction rises to the highest level. Customers are delighted by the consequence, increasing their loyalty to the company. A strategy which results in eliminating or minimizing wait lists for current best-selling books in a public library, for

Table 2.3

Attributes and Consequences for Select Library Services

SERVICE	ATTRIBUTE	CONSEQUENCE
Cataloging	Accurate, reliable	I found what I was looking for.
Circulation	Access	I was able to take the book home to work on my project.
Interlibrary Loan	Fast, efficient	I got a copy of the article I needed in two days!
Microforms	Staffed	A library employee saw my frustration and showed me how to use the microform printer so I could take the article home with me.
Website	24/7	I found an answer to my question at two o'clock in the morning and didn't have to leave my house!

Figure 2.2

The Kano Model

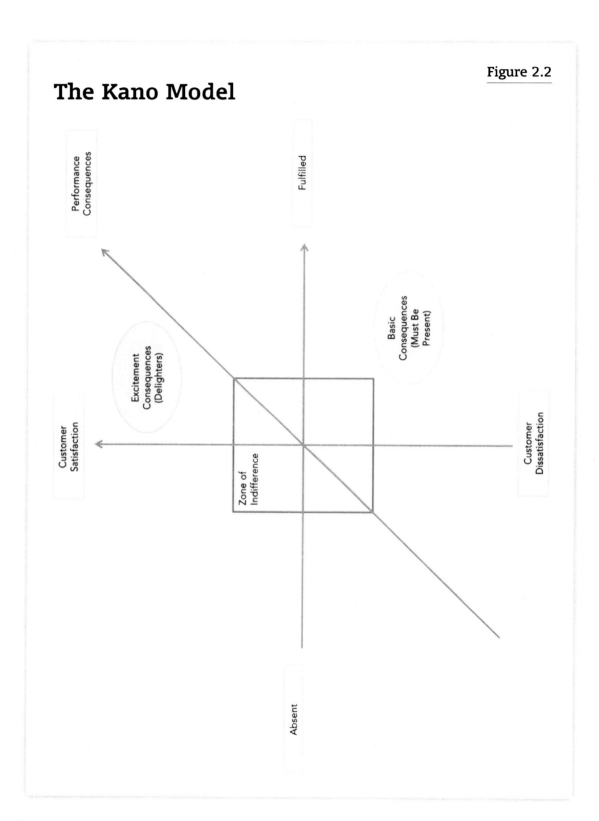

instance, may function as an excitement consequence, along with a robust genealogy program designed to assist local and visiting consumers with researching their family history.

Over time, as competitors adjust their operational strategies and products continue to evolve, excitement consequences become performance consequences or even basic consequences: expected, yet taken for granted within consumer groups. For library facilities, Internet access is one example. At one time, a library with Internet access and a functional website was a delighter for individuals without an Internet connection at home. Libraries are now expected to provide public access to current personal computing technology and the Internet. This is no longer an excitement or performance consequence, but rather a basic consequence that Western library consumers take for granted. This is in direct contrast to rural areas of developing countries, where having enough gasoline to run the town generator for four hours is a delighter, since it enables community members to use government-sponsored Internet cafes to connect to the outside world.

Since library and information consultants typically work in a larger library organization, it is especially important to have a formal process for gathering Voice of the Customer information and then ranking it to determine which consequences are of more importance to consumers than others. As with their peers outside of the library community, library and information consultants can tap into a variety of sources to both determine the attributes library consumers desire and the performance, excitement, and basic consequences that result from using library services. Such information can be gathered through interviews, focus groups, from fellow librarians' experiences working with consumers, observation, mystery shopping, or even open-ended survey questions. The main goal is to obtain an understanding of the consequences for using your service by listening to consumers' own words.

Once gathered, additional work must be done with consumers to sort and rank the importance of the consequences identified, especially because in the consumer's mind, not all consequences are weighted equally. For instance, the convenient location of a public branch library in relation to a consumer's home might not be as important to the consumer as the size of the library's main facility in a downtown location and the collection and services available at that facility. To begin sorting and ranking the consequences, the library and information consultant can construct an affinity diagram internally with colleagues or convene another focus group with library constituents for this next stage of the process.

Groups use affinity diagrams to list the ideas, opinions, and issues consumers identify and then organize them into groups based on their affinity or natural relationships. Figure 2.3 shows an affinity diagram created by a team of library and information consultants following a survey of library consumers. The survey asked open-ended questions designed to determine how the library could improve its services from the consumer's perspective. To create the affinity diagram, each member of the team reviewed the survey output, and then silently wrote each idea or issue he perceived the customer identified on an individual self-adhesive note. Team members are encouraged to use self-adhesive notes when creating affinity diagrams, to facilitate the grouping and regrouping of ideas. Once finished, each team member posted his self-adhesive notes on a wall, with the notes created by his teammates. Going around the room, each team member then silently grouped the notes in pairings that made sense to him. The goal for this stage of the affinity diagramming process is for team members to react quickly, grouping the ideas on instinct, rather than agonizing over choices. The grouping process is then repeated, until the participants agree on categories. This may take several rounds. When agreement is established, team members then collectively identify a consequence identified by each grouping to serve as a title for that category.

To elicit any consequences consumers may have overlooked, and to develop and translate the Voice of the Customer into quantifiable products and services, an internal brainstorming session with colleagues is called next, with the purpose of constructing a CTQC Tree. CTQC represents Critical to Quality Characteristics, or those actions or specific qualities of a service that can be quantified. Consumers often express their desires, needs, and wants in vague, general terms. The challenge for the service provider is then to translate these desires into performance standards or product specifications that will satisfy the consumer's needs. By constructing a CTQC Tree, the consultant can translate those difficult-to-measure, general needs expressed by the consumer into a more specific, easy-to-measure product or process that will satisfy the customer.

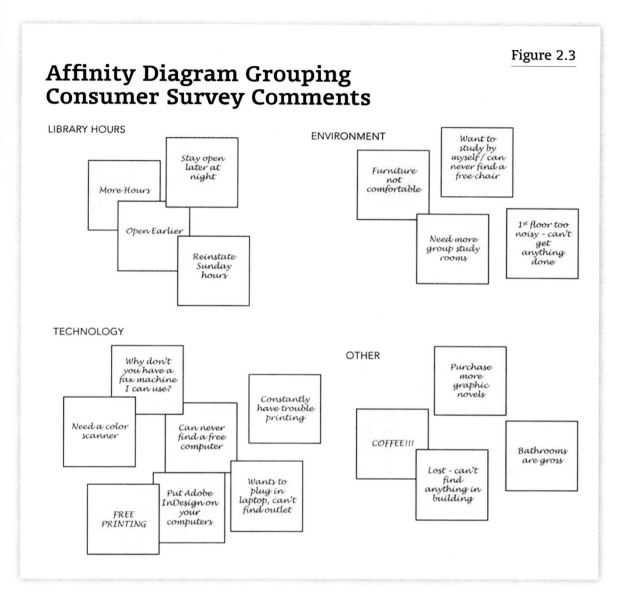

Figure 2.3

Affinity Diagram Grouping Consumer Survey Comments

LIBRARY HOURS

- Stay open later at night
- More Hours
- Open Earlier
- Reinstate Sunday hours

ENVIRONMENT

- Furniture not comfortable
- Want to study by myself / can never find a free chair
- Need more group study rooms
- 1st floor too noisy - can't get anything done

TECHNOLOGY

- Why don't you have a fax machine I can use?
- Need a color scanner
- Can never find a free computer
- Constantly have trouble printing
- FREE PRINTING
- Put Adobe InDesign on your computers
- Wants to plug in laptop, can't find outlet

OTHER

- Purchase more graphic novels
- COFFEE!!!
- Lost - can't find anything in building
- Bathrooms are gross

Figure 2.4 provides an example of a CTQC Tree constructed for a proactive library and information consulting service.[10] The customer's need for assistance where and when she needs it represents the Voice of the Customer data identified during the information gathering, affinity diagrams, or card sort process. The drivers represent the more specific tasks or elements that explain how to satisfy this consumer need. Drivers can be broken into subheadings that more specifically explain the meaning of the driver, if appropriate. For this example, drivers that influence customers' satisfaction with their ability to obtain information assistance where and when they need it include consultants who are easy to locate, easy to identify, and available to help. Lastly, to develop the CTQCs for each driver, the team asks, "What would this mean?" This forces the team to describe the performance standards or specifications for the product, service, or process that would function to satisfy the consumer's identified need. In this step, the team identifies the actionable, measurable characteristics of the service product or process. Measurable characteristics for a successful, proactive library and information consulting service in both a physical and online library environment are identified in figure 2.4.

Managing Service Experiences: Service Recovery

Once designed and implemented, service experiences must be managed. Every interaction a customer has with a service may be described as a moment of truth, and the consumer's perception of the service provided can be described as a function of all of his previous moments of truth. Thus, while it is important to design a service product or process with the Voice of the Customer in mind, execution of the service is equally important. As noted earlier, customer loyalty increases with customer satisfaction. The key to building and maintaining customer relationships is to excite and delight customers. Those who perceive your service exceeded their basic performance expectations will more likely return to utilize your services and recommend your services to others. Unfortunately, a poor experience can negatively affect a customer's collective moments of truth, causing the organization to lose the customer's esteem and loyalty. Thus library and information consultants must manage the environment around them, recognizing that episodes of service failure are inevitable, especially as many factors influencing the provision of service, such as weather-related building closings or customer moods, cannot be controlled. This means plans for service recovery must be built into the design of the service product or process.[11]

The backbone of any plan for service recovery is the establishment of customer feedback loops. After all, if you don't know the customer was dissatisfied, how can you remedy the situation? In a library setting, this

Figure 2.4

CTQC Tree for a Proactive Library and Information Consulting Service

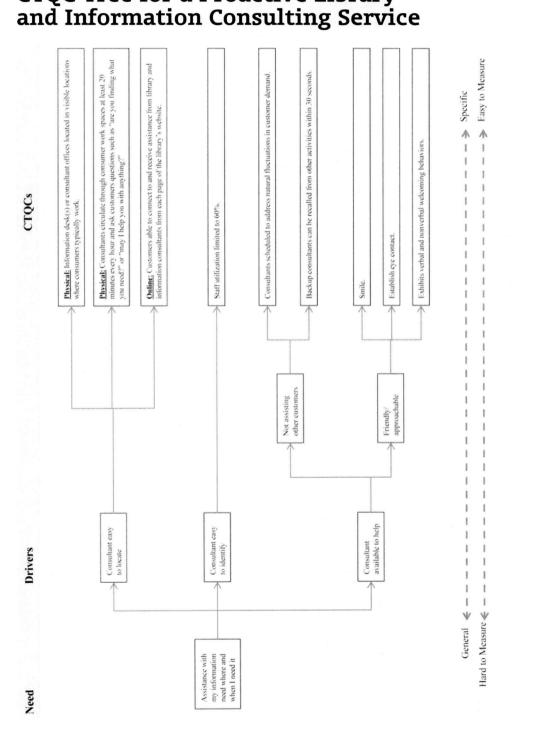

means collecting customer comment cards, establishing an online form or telephone number for complaints, interviewing both current and lost customers, or establishing an ombudsman to investigate complaints. Plans and procedures for reporting and addressing anticipated service failures, such as computer network outages, or collection unavailability due to building repairs, are necessary to address potential sources for customer dissatisfaction before and immediately after they occur.

Quickly corrected service failures are less likely to reap the customer's disfavor, meaning library and information consultants must be prepared, trained, and empowered to handle problems. Creativity, decisiveness, and effective communication skills are essential. Consultants trained and empowered to address service failures are also required. The goal of any service recovery plan is for each and every library and information consultant to achieve closure with the customer when service failure occurs or at least be able to provide an explanation to the customer on why the situation cannot be addressed.

Summary

With an understanding of the factors influencing service process design and the process for identifying the Voice of the Customer, library and information consultants can attract new clients to their services and maintain existing consumer relationships. The intangible nature of services makes them extremely difficult to define and quantify. An understanding of a library organization's service-product bundle, along with the degree of customer interaction and product customization required, is necessary to successfully design and implement a service process.

If a service does not meet a customer's expectations, the customer will seek viable alternatives to the same service. Thus the service provider must remain focused on the Voice of the Customer. The process for identifying the Voice of the Customer not only involves the gathering of data, but the translation of this data into actionable, measurable performance standards or specifications that will satisfy the consumer's expressed need. The challenge for the library and information consultant is that customer expectations continuously change over time. A performance characteristic that was once a delighter will eventually become a customer expectation. Tools such as the affinity diagram, card sorts, and the CTQC tree can help the consultant to develop and translate Voice of the Customer data gathered through surveys, focus groups, and other mechanisms into programs that satisfy consumer needs.

Although proper execution of a newly designed service is also necessary to satisfy customer expectations, service failure will occasionally occur, as managers cannot control all factors affecting the consumer's service experience. Where possible, plans and procedures for quick and effective service recovery must be designed into the service process. Library and information consultants working for a library organization must also be empowered to address consumer complaints as they arise.

Notes

1. James A. Fitzsimmons and Mona J. Fitzsimmons, *Service Management: Operations, Strategy, Information Technology* (Boston: McGraw-Hill/Irwin, 2008).
2. Roger G. Schroeder, *Operations Management: Contemporary Concepts and Cases* (Boston: McGraw-Hill/Irwin, 2007).
3. Scott Bennett, "First Questions for Designing Higher Education Learning Spaces," *Journal of Academic Librarianship* 33, no. 1 (January 2007): 14–26; Scott Bennett, "Designing for Uncertainty: Three Approaches," *Journal of Academic Librarianship* 33, no. 2 (March 2007): 165–79.
4. Bonnie A. Nardi and Vicki O'Day, *Information Ecologies: Using Technology with Heart* (Cambridge, MA: MIT Press, 1999).
5. Ruth Vondracek, "Comfort and Convenience? Why Students Choose Alternatives to the Library," *portal: Libraries and the Academy* 7, no. 3 (July 2007): 277–93.
6. Susan M. Keaveney, "Customer Switching Behavior in Service Industries: An Exploratory Study," *Journal of Marketing* 59, no. 2 (April 1995): 71–82.
7. Richard Metters, Kathryn King-Metters, and Madeleine Pullman, *Successful Service Operations Management* (Mason, OH: South-Western, 2003): 81.
8. iSixSigma, "Voice of the Customer (VOC)," www.isixsigma.com/index.php?option =com_glossary&id=327&Itemid=228.
9. Caroline M. Fisher and James T. Schutta, *Developing New Services: Incorporating the Voice of the Customer into Strategic Service Development* (Milwaukee, WI: ASQ Quality Press, 2003).
10. Rath and Strong, *Rath and Strong's Six Sigma Pocket Guide* (Lexington, MA: Rath and Strong Management Consultants, 2006).
11. *Successful Service Operations Management,* 150–51.

3

Marketing the Library and Information Consultant's Services

Creating a Sophisticated Brand

Quality marketing of professional services is both an art and a science, requiring careful research by consultants to identify, retain, and grow a dedicated clientele. As customers continually exercise their right to choose, consultants must deliver value through their professional services and consistently communicate the value of those services to current and potential clients. Librarians often mistake marketing as advertising and publicity, which are just two of many tools or tactics in the marketing arsenal. True marketing is a managerial process, or, as stated by the American Marketing Association, "an organizational function and set of processes for creating, communicating, and delivering value to customers and for managing customer relationships in ways that benefit the organization and its stakeholders."[1] By listening and responding to the voice of the customer, the library and information consultant can craft a sophisticated marketing strategy.

This chapter focuses on marketing the library and information consultant's services, with the goal of creating a brand identity that library consumers can both relate to and value. It will begin with an introduction to services marketing, discussing the value of the ServiceScape for effectively marketing a professional service product and the service blueprint for managing it. It will continue by outlining the traditional marketing plan, used for articulating the professional service product's value. The chapter will end with a discussion on branding and the integrated marketing communications plan, as a means to consistently communicate the value of a library and information consultant's professional services.

Services Marketing

To review, service products differ considerably from physical goods. Most notably they are heterogeneous and intangible in nature, requiring performances from both employees and the consumer. These characteristics lead to inherent variability in operational inputs and outputs, making services extremely difficult for customers to understand, let alone evaluate.

Customers, regardless of the degree of intangible service they've purchased, usually rely on tangible, or physical, evidence to judge service quality. Thus the discipline of marketing services is integrated with service operations. When visiting a grocery store, for example, the customer views the display of produce, the cleanliness of the bathrooms, the quality of aisle and pricing signage, and the friendliness of checkout clerks as clues regarding the quality of both the store and their service experience. This means a visit to Whole Foods, where employees are available to assist customers with matching seafood with varieties of fine wine, is very different than a visit to ALDI, where a "less is more philosophy" means customer interaction with employees is minimized. In the library setting, the consumer is accessing the library and information consultant's knowledge when asking a question. It is unlikely that the consumer will base his opinion of the success of a reference transaction on whether the consultant responded to his question with the perfect answer alone. Rather the entire ServiceScape of the library will be included in the consumer's assessment. To provide and market a service product consistently, the consultant needs to understand and develop his organization's ServiceScape and construct a service blueprint so that he can objectively and quantifiably manage his service product.

ServiceScape

ServiceScape represents the environment in which a service is delivered and customers interact with employees.[2] A ServiceScape is an important concern, because it influences both customer and employee behavior. Before, during, and after a customer uses a service, the customer will consider the physical evidence and use this evidence to formulate his opinion of that service. Thus building characteristics such as the quality of furnishings, building layout, signage, and equipment will communicate both quality and value to the customer along with other tangibles, such as the consistent presentation of brochures, websites, and other communication mediums. Ideally a ServiceScape satisfies the needs of both the consumer and the library and information consultant. It should be designed with the marketing segments the consultant wishes to target. The Columbus Metropolitan Library in Columbus, Ohio, for instance, offers Job Help Centers. These centers are physically located in its branch locations and defined using signage and furniture. To assist community members looking for work, it also partners with JOB*Leaders*, a statewide organization, to bring the Jobs Mobile bus to its locations.[3] This is a significant element of the Columbus Metropolitan Library's ServiceScape in a state with countywide unemployment rates reaching 7 to 16 percent.[4]

Similarly, the Veria Central Public Library in Greece created "The Magic Boxes," a space within its library designed to promote reading, creativity, and digital literacy for its community's children.[5] To enable children to interact with one another and express their creativity and curiosity, the Veria library intentionally made this ServiceScape flexible, with multipurpose furniture that can continuously be reconfigured. It also selected colors and materials that will engage children's emotions and creativity.

The complexity of a library's ServiceScape, however, can overwhelm consumers. This is an undeniable reality today as collections and services are now spread throughout a physical and online environment. A visitor to the Thompson Library at The Ohio State University, for example, initially encounters collections and services spread over an eleven-floor building with more than two hundred thousand assignable square feet of space. Signage alone is insufficient to help the visitor navigate this space. All staff must consciously interact with consumers in the building who appear lost or confused, offering directions or physically escorting the consumer to her desired destination. To help visitors, standards of employee dress, such as Vocera communication badges worn with traditional picture identification badges, are employed to distinguish staff from regular patrons.[6] Vocera communication badges further shape the ServiceScape by assisting staff with addressing consumers' information needs at their time and place of need. Part phone, part pager, part walkie-talkie, Vocera uses voice commands to enable staff to communicate with each other regardless of where they are in a building. Thus, if a consumer on the tenth floor of the Thompson Library approaches an employee shelving books with a detailed question, this employee can immediately call a library and information consultant for help, without having to physically escort the consumer to a phone or a consultant's office. Vocera also allows users to call groups; a circulation supervisor can send employees to work on a shifting project in the stacks knowing that she may use Vocera to summon these individuals back to the desk if a line forms. These standards contribute to the ServiceScape.

The Thompson Library, however, is just one building in a system of eight department libraries, six regional campus libraries, separately administered law and health sciences libraries, and a remote storage facility. Ohio State library consumers can borrow materials from or make use of any of these facilities. The Ohio State Libraries' ServiceScape is further complicated as their customers can request books and journals through the statewide OhioLINK system, a consortium of eighty-eight Ohio college and university libraries and the State Library of Ohio. To address this issue the Ohio State Libraries employs a communications officer and a graphic designer, who work in tandem to craft carefully designed maps, brochures, websites, and other media to assist patrons with understanding the Ohio State library system. This is an important yet daunting task, as is communicating a consistent message regarding the Ohio State Libraries. It is an important contribution to the ServiceScape, however, influencing consumers' commitment to the library system, their use of library services, whether they recommend the library to their peers, and whether they support the library's funding.

The ServiceScape also enables customers to differentiate one area of service from another within the library. Using furniture, private consultation rooms and other elements, a library and information consultant may distinguish her service area from others, such as circulation or a technology help center. Further, placement of computer terminals and chairs in the areas where a library and information consultant interacts with customers will affect social interaction. If chairs are placed so far away that the consultant cannot hear the consumer, the ServiceScape will be negatively affected.

While the ServiceScape facilitates the performance of both consumers and library employees, it also socializes them by communicating roles, behaviors, and relationships. The ServiceScape may define the role of the library and information consultant by functioning as a differentiator that both attracts and repels market segments. A well-trained, knowledgeable consultant, for instance, will not be able to encourage highly educated customers to use her services if her behavior contradicts her knowledge. Locating patron answers while blowing large bubbles with green-apple-scented chewing gum, for instance, may distract the consumer and communicate a lack of respect for the consumer's question.

Because customer decisions to use or avoid a library service are influenced by staff, hiring, retention, and promotion decisions also contribute to the ServiceScape. Having the right employee in the right position influences customer decisions to stay and use a service as much as environmental conditions such a natural lighting, noise, and building temperature. Friendly library and information consultants who display both verbal and physical welcoming behaviors will be more successful than knowledgeable library and information consultants who repel potential clients with dismissive facial expressions.

The ServiceScape's physical environment also affects staff behavior cognitively, emotionally, and physiologically. If a work area is in front of an open door during a cold northern winter, this can negatively impact even the most talented library and information consultant. The consultant must ask herself whether a consumer would enjoy an interaction in such a setting. If the consultant is uncomfortable, the consumer is likely uncomfortable too! Failure to address the uncomfortable environment will lead to avoidance behaviors from both the consultant and the consumer whom the consultant wishes to attract.

Service Blueprinting

The less experienced the consumer, the more important it is for the service provider to manage the consumer's service experience. Service blueprinting complements the ServiceScape by detailing the processes and specifications to which the service product should conform. Introduced by G. Lynn Shostack, a former vice-president at Citibank and chair of the American Marketing Association's special task force on service marketing, the service blueprint maps the processes inherent in a service and identifies potential points of failure by indicating all potential points of contact where the customer and service provider interact.[7] It is a useful tool for developing or improving a new or existing service. By understanding potential failure points, the library and information consultant can either address the service failure by redesigning the service process, or, if appropriate, create contingency plans to minimize or address a service failure that cannot be avoided. For instance, in a library that offers a series of popular classes requiring pre-registration, unavoidable service failure may occur on the first day of registration, particularly if budgetary realities restrict the library to accepting registrations by telephone only. If telephone capacity cannot be increased to address the increased volume of calls from eager consumers, a service failure will occur.

There are various formats of the service blueprint an organization can use. It is best to choose a format that works best for the consultant's professional service products and to use this format consistently. An example of a service blueprint for a proactive library and information consulting service is provided in figure 3.1. To construct this blueprint, the key activities required to produce and deliver the service from the customer's and consultant's points of view were identified first and mapped into the following categories of actions: customer actions, employee actions both onstage and backstage, and support processes. The tangible physical evidence the customer experiences for the service process was also identified and recorded at the top of the blueprint. The service blueprint illustrates that front room and back room activities run in parallel. Along with the physical evidence, these activities contribute to the successful delivery of the service.

In figure 3.1, the author attempted to identify all of the steps taken, frustrations experienced, and choices made by a library customer looking for articles on a specific topic. The onstage and backstage actions taken by the consultant interacting with a customer in a proactive library and information consulting service are listed. Backstage activities include anything that the contact employee does to assist the customer onstage. Lastly, the support processes that aid the contact employee in delivering the service are listed. In a library organization, this would include activities conducted by individuals in acquisitions, cataloging, information technology, and general management.

As composed, the service blueprint denotes three key action areas: the line of interaction, the line of visibility, and the line of internal interaction. Service encounters are denoted any time a vertical line crosses the line of interaction; this means a customer has interacted with an employee. The

Blueprint for Proactive Library and Information Consulting Service

Figure 3.1

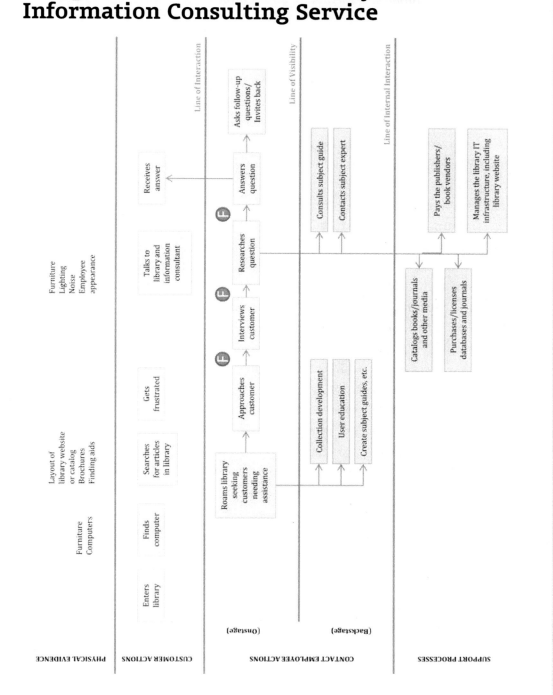

PHYSICAL EVIDENCE

- Furniture
- Computers

- Layout of library website or catalog
- Brochures
- Finding aids

- Furniture
- Lighting
- Noise
- Employee appearance

CUSTOMER ACTIONS

- Enters library
- Finds computer
- Searches for articles in library
- Gets frustrated
- Talks to library and information consultant
- Receives answer

Line of Interaction

CONTACT EMPLOYEE ACTIONS

(Onstage)

- Roams library seeking customers needing assistance
- Approaches customer
- Interviews customer
- Researches question
- Answers question
- Asks follow-up questions / Invites back

(Backstage)

- Collection development
- User education
- Create subject guides, etc.

- Consults subject guide
- Contacts subject expert

Line of Visibility

SUPPORT PROCESSES

- Catalogs books/journals and other media
- Purchases/licenses databases and journals

- Pays the publishers/book vendors
- Manages the library IT infrastructure, including library website

Line of Internal Interaction

45

line of visibility denotes all activities which are visible to the customer and on which the customer will formulate an opinion of her individual service experience. This includes everything above the line of interaction. Potential failure points are usually identified above this line and represented by a circled capital F. Making a service process more visible to the customer or improving the physical evidence can sometimes address these failure points. In other instances, a redesign of the service process may be required. For example, in an academic library setting, offering tours of a remote storage facility to university faculty and graduate students can help manage expectations regarding book retrieval wait times. Circulating a short YouTube video explaining this facility to these target populations may also creatively accomplish this task. Changing the process for retrieving items in a way that reduces wait time is also an option.

Vertical lines that cross the line of internal interaction represent internal service encounters. This would include contacts consultants make with colleagues in information technology. A request for assistance with creating and posting a subject guide in the library organization's content management system, for example, is not seen by the customer. Completion of this activity, however, is required for a successful service transaction.

To improve a service or address failure points, any activities identified in the service blueprint may require a service blueprint of its own. The beauty of the service blueprint, however, is that each service encounter identified by the vertical lines indicates a "moment of truth." Here an internal or external customer may have an excellent or poor service experience. The service blueprint illustrates that service failure is usually not a factor of human error but a lack of systematic design and control. The blueprint provides an opportunity to systematically describe a service concept and record detailed specifications. It represents the who, what, where, when, and how of the service product. The service blueprint represented in figure 3.1 shows three potential failure points: when the consultant approaches and interviews the customer; when the consultant researches the customer's question; and when the consultant gives the customer an answer and follows up with a question or invitation to return for additional service. These failures will not occur in every transaction. In fact, they may rarely occur at all. The service blueprint, however, prompts library and information consultants to honestly work toward minimizing errors in their service, through such practices as training or standardizing practice. From a marketing perspective, the service blueprint is essential for understanding a service and creating both a marketing plan and a brand identity to communicate its value.

The Marketing Plan: A Foundation for Articulating Value

Successful marketing is embedded in the design, creation, and implementation of products and services. It is not an activity undertaken after a good or service is created. Since marketing primarily focuses on value creation and delivery, it is vital for any library and information consultant to have a sound strategy for researching the needs of current and potential customers. With the information gathered from the ServiceScape, service blueprinting, and Voice of the Customer tools and activities, the consultant can obtain precise knowledge of customer needs. Using this knowledge, he can successfully create both services and products that meet these needs and communicate the value of these services and products. The consultant can then create a marketing plan to commit his understanding of the marketplace, with its various segments, competitors, and overall environment, in writing. The purpose of the marketing plan is to identify target populations, objectives for the marketing program, a positioning strategy, and the mix of advertisements and promotional strategies to be used to communicate with the target population. Measurable financial or behavioral outcomes along with a strategy for implementing and adjusting the marketing strategy are also identified. These adjustments are accomplished by establishing internal controls and external measures to inform decision making.

While many formats of the marketing plan exist and are advocated by experts, a well-crafted marketing plan consists of strategies and tactics. The strategic component focuses on the value proposition to be created and delivered after analyzing a market environment. The tactical component focuses on specific marketing tools or methods, such as promotion, pricing, or service features, to communicate the value proposition to the markets targeted. Most marketing plans consist of six basic elements:

1. a *situation/market analysis* which examines the product or consultant's current strengths, weaknesses, opportunities, and threats in the broader marketplace. This is often referred to as a SWOT analysis.

2. a *customer analysis* that answers key questions about current customers' or prospects' decision-making influences

3. *marketing goals and objectives* stated in measurable terms

4. a *marketing strategy* outlining the tactics required to achieve these goals

5. a *budget* which supports the marketing strategy

6. an *execution and evaluation plan* for implementing and adjusting the marketing strategy

The situation and market analysis ground the marketing plan by requiring examination of the overall macroenvironment. The customer analysis, marketing goals and objectives, and marketing strategy focus on the value proposition. The budget and evaluation plan are necessary to measure the plan's effectiveness. More formal marketing plans are usually prefaced by an executive summary, which highlights key points from each segment of the document.

Situation/Market Analysis

Any strengths, weaknesses, opportunities, and threats relevant to the library and information consultant's professional service products are documented in the situation analysis. Strengths include anything from having a team of highly knowledgeable, effective, and experienced employees, to having a unique product or service that cannot easily be replicated by others. Weaknesses include factors such as limited funding opportunities or a hiring freeze that compromises the consultant's ability to replace valued employees following retirement. Opportunities represent external factors that the consultant can capitalize upon to improve value creation and delivery to consumers, while threats represent external environmental factors the consultant may not be able to control, but can address to minimize the disruption to or interference with a product or service.

Any factor that may influence usage of the consultant's services must be considered in the situation analysis. For instance, the economic downturn of 2008–2009 reinforced the relationship between a weakening economy and usage of libraries, particularly library programs and resources related to job seeking in areas of high unemployment. It also highlighted public libraries' reliance on state and local tax revenues for daily operation and support. Other legal and governmental factors such as copyright or local building and fire code compliance must be documented in the situation analysis, as these issues will influence the overall marketing strategy of a library and information consultant. Technological and sociocultural trends, such as social networking, Web 2.0, or mobile broadband, must also be documented in the situation analysis section of the marketing plan.

In the market analysis, current and potential competitors, their influence in the marketplace, and how this influence may affect the market are examined. Here competitors' strengths and weaknesses are identified, with detail illustrating how they may affect delivery or use of the consultant's professional service products. Information about the market environment is also documented in the market analysis, including specific market circumstances that the consultant may or may not be able to control.

Customer Analysis

Both current and potential markets for the consultant's professional service products are documented in the customer analysis. This is accomplished by defining the size of the market and the various segments within the market. Market segments represent groups of customers who share similar needs, desires, and preferences. An understanding of these groups may be used to focus various marketing strategies and tactics. Marketers usually segment consumer markets broadly by the following variables:

- *geographic,* including factors such as where current and potential clients live, or where they spend the majority of their time
- *demographic,* including factors that classify consumers into groups based on variables such as age, sex, income, and highest educational level obtained
- *psychographic,* including psychological, lifestyle, personality, or any behavioral traits groups of consumers may have in common

With psychological segmentation, the consultant can look at such things as decision roles. This includes who influences an individual's decision to use a library and information consultant's services. Thus, the library and information consultant can examine what psychological factors encourage students to study in a library and at what time of day. Physical and psychological factors, such as a consultant colocated in an academic library coffee bar or a safe place for kids to get help with their homework in the public library, encourage a consumer to utilize a library and information consultant's services repeatedly, and refer these services to a friend. Such referrals are especially important as word-of-mouth marketing is not only free, but extremely effective. Although much of the information for segmenting has already been collected while defining the Voice of the Customer, it is important to document measurable market segments in the marketing plan, because this information is necessary to define which markets to target both for the design and promotion of the consultant's service product.

Marketing Goals and Objectives

Once background information has been collected and documented to inform the marketing plan, the strategies and tactics are outlined next. Marketing goals and objectives must be stated in measurable terms. This requires defining target markets using the information documented earlier in the market segmentation, to focus the consultant's financial, capital, and human resources on potential customers. These are individuals who are most receptive to using and appreciating the value of the consultant's products and services. The marketing goals and objectives must also be linked to the consultant's stated mission. Thus, if the overarching mission of the library is to promote literacy and lifelong learning within its community, a consultant's target market might include adults age thirty and older with school-age children living within five miles of the North Everett branch. Note that the geographic and demographic variables for this target market are clearly defined. Parents of school-age children influence their child's ability to use the library and the library's services. If the goal of the consultant's marketing plan is to encourage individuals in this target market, whose tax dollars both contribute to and support the library's mission, the marketing objectives may be:

- increase the number of families attending weekly storytelling programs sponsored by the North Everett branch
- improve parents' recognition of the North Everett branch as a source for parenting, health, and other information
- increase the number of K–8 students using the North Everett branch homework help program

Marketing Strategy

To create a marketing strategy, the consultant must articulate a positioning strategy for a product, service, or brand by outlining marketing's traditional four Ps. The four Ps represent the marketing mix and encourage the library and information consultant to balance the marketing strategy by considering the:

- *product* or the benefits the customer receives from utilizing the product or service, the product's relationship to other products, services, and brands already marketed by the library organization, and factors such as product quality, design, or features
- *price,* defined as the product or service's published price, or factors such as payment terms and financing, discounts, or terms of credit
- *place (distribution)* or the variables outlining where, when, and how consumers will be able to utilize the product or service
- *promotion,* which includes the various mechanisms for communicating the value of a product or service to consumers through advertising, sales promotions, direct marketing, events, public relations, personal sales, and the Internet

Some marketers add an additional three categories to the four Ps for service products including:

- *process* or the policies, training, and standards that define how the service product is to be delivered to consumers and how customer satisfaction is measured and/or monitored
- *physical evidence* of the service product, which includes factors such as the environment in which the service is delivered

- *people* or the individuals the organization or consultant hires to deliver the service product

As noted in chapter 2, categories such as price may be defined more broadly, including variables such as the price of convenience or the price of receiving inaccurate information.

The point of the marketing strategy is to highlight the points of difference and points of parity between a product and a competitor's product in an effort to influence consumers' choices.[8] Points of difference represent the attributes or benefits a product or service offers the consumer that the consumer believes cannot be obtained from a competitor. For the service product, this may include the format of the service, features, performance quality, reliability, and style. The ability to locate a specific children's book for a customer without having a title or author, for instance, often serves as a point of difference between a library and information consultant and a bookstore employee. Points of parity represent the attributes or benefits a product or service offers that the consumer can satisfy elsewhere. This may also include elements of the service format, features, performance quality, reliability, and style. Points of parity are not necessarily negative. If a consumer expects your product or service to offer similar elements as a competitor's service, failure to meet these expectations can influence the consumer to choose a competitor's product or service. Thus if a bookstore offers premium coffee in its café, and the library's coffee kiosk does not, the coffee aficionados will choose the bookstore over the library for study space. Points of parity and points of difference must be relevant, distinctive, and believable to adequately influence consumer behavior. They must also be feasible, able to be communicated, and sustainable for the consultant or organization that establishes them.

Budget

The expected costs for implementing the marketing plan are identified in detail in the budget section of the marketing plan. Here the financial resources required for advertising and promotional activities are outlined, along with any costs associated with evaluating the marketing plan's success in meeting its goals and objectives, such as hiring an independent survey research group. Although the typical marketing plan should include a sales forecast to predict expected revenue and a break-even analysis to identify the point where profits will be realized, this may or may not be appropriate for the library and information consultant. If the consultant were marketing a fundraising event, the projected fundraising goal would serve as the sales forecast from which the forecasted costs to market and execute the program would be subtracted to determine the program's break-even point. For a grant-funded program, however, determining the break-even point may prove more difficult. With no exchange of financial resources, community outcomes or outputs may prove more relevant. Thus, for a community with a 10 percent unemployment rate, the library and information consultant's sales forecast for a grant-funded job-seeking assistance program may instead be defined as "10 percent of our community's unemployed citizens will attend one of the library's ten resume-writing workshops within the next three months."

Execution and Evaluation Plan

A marketing plan has no strength unless a detailed timetable for executing each individual marketing activity is created and followed. The consultant must identify both mechanisms and dates for measuring the overall success of the marketing plan and adjusting its implementation. Having a detailed execution and evaluation plan not only improves accountability, both internally and externally, but also the success of the marketing campaign.

Branding the Library and Information Consultant's Service Product

Branding solidifies the image the library and information consultant wishes to portray for his professional service products, and is a valuable tool for both conveying the value of these services and differentiating them from the services offered by others. Branding tells a story, helping consumers to understand what they might expect when using service. Well-executed branding strategies generate equity for a consultant, influencing how consumers will think, feel, and react. A strong brand appeals to a consumer's emotions and creates a loyal customer willing to invest more time, money, and resources in her service experience. It establishes a presence for the service product, communicates its relevance to the consumer, and assures the consumer that the product will deliver what it promises. The goal of branding is to move consumers from simply identifying a brand and knowing that it exists, to associating a brand with their needs. A loyal consumer will become a passionate brand supporter, developing a lasting bond with the brand.

Branding is more holistic than logos and letterhead. A strong brand will communicate and reflect how a library and information consultant does business. Thus development of a marketing plan, a series of service blueprints, and an understanding of a ServiceScape all contribute to the creation and maintenance of a sophisticated brand. A strong brand is memorable, meaningful, likeable, transferable, adaptable, and protectable.[9] This means brand names for the library and information consultant's professional service products, along with visual representations of the consultant's brand via logos and websites, taglines, and other marketing tools, must support the brand's promise. To accomplish this, the library and information consultant must work with his organization's integrated marketing communications strategy, or insist that one must be employed, to consistently communicate his brand's promise while protecting and strengthening his brand's image.

An integrated marketing communications strategy considers how all advertising, promotional, public relations, and other marketing activities work together to support the brand image. It requires coordinating the visual identity for a brand and establishing set standards for using the brand. For the library and information consultant, this means an editorial policy for the brand must be created and executed. All employees must understand and respect standards that define elements, such as how the brand will be referred to in writing and whether certain documents must be forwarded to a brand advocate for approval before distribution. For example, the author is currently employed by The Ohio State University. Here she is required to refer to the institution as "The Ohio State University" the first time the university is referred to in written documents. Subsequent references must be written as "Ohio State," not "OSU," with the word university un-capitalized. Employees are referred to the 15th edition of the *Chicago Manual of Style* for editorial issues not addressed by the university's editorial style guide.[10]

Design standards must also be employed in tandem with editorial standards. Design standards define the basic rules for how the visual elements, such as logos, colors, or templates for a brand, must be employed. To coordinate and monitor the execution of editorial and design standards for an integrated marketing communications strategy, the appointment of a brand champion or advocate is often necessary. This individual functions as the "voice of the brand" and must lead regular brand audits to ensure the library and information consultant's message is consistent and successful in triggering a desired emotional response from targeted consumers. If no individual within the library organization has been appointed to this role, the library and information consultant must either consciously serve as his own brand advocate, or insist that the library appoint someone to oversee the entire organization's branding efforts.

Summary

Library and information consultants must craft a sophisticated marketing strategy to successfully communicate the value of their professional services to current and future customers. The consultant must understand the ServiceScape or environment in which his service products are delivered, as customers rely on tangible evidence to evaluate the quality of these services. This means library and information consultants must ensure that such details as furnishings, decor, written communications, and employee behavior and dress all match the value proposition of their professional service products.

The discipline of creating service blueprints supports the library and information consultant's efforts to create and maintain an appropriate ServiceScape by detailing the processes and specifications to which their service products must conform. Service blueprints may also assist with identifying and addressing potential points in a service process where failure may occur.

With a written marketing plan, the library and information consultant may articulate the value of his professional service products to customers. The marketing plan assists the consultant by forcing the consultant to identify and then segment target populations, create a positioning strategy, and determine the mix of advertising and promotional activities required to successfully communicate the value of a service to the target populations. A quality marketing plan identifies measurable financial or behavioral outcomes to enable the consultant to monitor the plan's success and adjust the plan as necessary.

Lastly, branding generates equity, creating loyal customers by appealing to customer emotions. Loyal customers not only invest a considerable amount of time, energy, and resources into a brand, but they also sell a brand to others. A consultant should either function as an advocate for the brand himself or appoint an individual to serve in this capacity. This ensures the consultant's professional service product delivers what it promises.

Notes

1. American Marketing Association, "Resource Library: Dictionary," www.marketing power.com/_layouts/Dictionary.aspx?dLetter=M.
2. Mary Jo Bitner, "ServiceScapes: The Impact of Physical Surroundings on Customers and Employees," *Journal of Marketing* 56, no. 2 (1992): 57–71.
3. Columbus Metropolitan Library, "Job Help Center," www.columbuslibrary.org/job help.
4. Ohio Department of Job and Family Services, "July 2010 Ranking of Ohio County Unemployment Rates," http://lmi.state.oh.us/LAUS/Ranking.pdf.
5. Veria Central Public Library, "The Magic Boxes," http://blog.libver.gr/en/?page_id=26.
6. Sarah Anne Murphy, "Vocera: Enhancing Communication across a Library System," *College and Research Libraries News* 70, no. 7 (2009): 408–11.
7. G. L. Shostack, "Designing Services That Deliver," *Harvard Business Review* 62, no. 1 (1984): 133–39.
8. Philip Kotler and Kevin Lane Keller, *Marketing Management,* 12th ed. (Upper Saddle River, NJ: Pearson Prentice Hall, 2006), 312–16.
9. Ibid., 282.
10. The Ohio State University. "Office of Marketing Communications, Editorial Style Guide," www.osu.edu.proxy.lib.ohio-state.edu/resources/styleguide.html.

The Business of Consulting

Managing Employee Service Roles and Consumer Demand

ny good manual on consulting will focus on mastering the resource management required for a successful practice, such as managing your cash flow, investing in your employees, and making strategic capital improvements. This also applies to the library environment. As stewards of the financial resources provided by a municipal, university, or grant-making organization, a library and information consultant must allocate his financial, capital, and human resources in the most efficient and effective manner possible. Although profit may not be the motivating factor driving the library and information consultant's services, successfully making a difference in the lives of consumers is.

This chapter focuses on managing employee service roles and customer demand as a means for delivering service products and programs that successfully address customer expectations and perceptions. It begins by briefly introducing the Integrated Gaps Model of Service Quality. The Gaps model provides a framework for discussing the complex, interrelated skill sets, activities, and strategies required for successfully matching the service a consumer actually receives with the service she expected to receive. It then examines employee roles in the delivery of library and information consulting services and the imperative need to hire, develop, empower, and retain the right people for delivering the service product. A discussion on the management of consultant supply with consumer demand follows, along with the psychology of waits, as this directly impacts customer satisfaction. Finally the chapter concludes with a discussion on the importance of impact evaluation and its role in the strategic allocation of financial and capital resources.

The Library and Information Consultant: Managing Employee Service Roles

Consumers often enter a service establishment expecting to receive one level of service, only to leave disappointed because the service they actually received failed to meet their expectations. The Integrated Gaps Model of Service Quality provides a means for framing the activities required and skill sets needed to successfully address this disconnect between customer expectations and perceptions and the actual service provided. Used by service marketers, the Gaps model acknowledges that firms must close the overarching gap between what customers expect and what customers actually receive.[1] To close this gap, four additional interrelated gaps must first be addressed. These gaps include:

- Gap 1: failure to match the organization's perception of customer expectations with customer's actual expectations
- Gap 2: failure to select service designs and standards that address the organization's perception of customer expectations
- Gap 3: failure to meet the service designs and standards established by the organization in the delivery of the service
- Gap 4: failure to deliver the service promised to customers

Gaps 1 and 2, which result from not knowing what customers actually expect and not having the right service designs and standards to address these expectations, were addressed in chapters 2 and 3 of this book. An understanding of the Voice of the Customer, for instance, is imperative for translating customer expectations appropriately into relevant service products. Marketing activities not only communicate the value of a service product to the customer, but can also manage customer expectations and perceptions by educating the consumer on what to expect from the service product, including its benefits and limitations.

Gap 3 is often referred to as the performance gap. The most frequent contribution to this gap, or the failure to meet service designs and standards, is poor management of human resources. This is also true for gap 4, failing to deliver a service as promised to customers. To successfully close gaps 3 and 4, the library and information consultant must successfully manage employee service roles.

Employees interacting directly with the public have some of the most demanding positions in any service industry. Because they serve as the face of the product, it is critical for employees to perform or deliver services at the level of quality promised to the customer. Working within library organizations, library and information consultants function in what the industry considers *boundary-spanning* positions.[2] These are roles in which the consultant not only personifies the service itself, but must function as a marketer, operations specialist, advisor, and sometimes leader. Internal personal conflict may arise as the consultant struggles to satisfy the customer, the library organization, and himself. This may be downright impossible, especially when having to address a consumer's unrealistic expectations. A consultant interacting with a consumer through a library chat or IM service, for instance, may experience considerable frustration when trying to assist a consumer with an ill-defined information need. After repeated attempts to clarify the consumer's question fail and an invitation to speak over the phone is dismissed by the consumer, the consultant may be internally screaming, "Just ask the question!" or "Pick up the phone please so that I can help you!" Positions must be designed carefully to mitigate this conflict. Further, the right individuals must be selected for these roles, as employee satisfaction is closely intertwined with customer satisfaction. Stressed, burned-out consultants can compromise the quality of the service product, resulting in increased customer dissatisfaction. Satisfied consultants, however, generate a positive circle of satisfaction by producing satisfied customers. These satisfied customers, in turn, produce satisfied employees, especially for those employees with a strong inclination for service provision.

The real-time decision making required of individuals serving in boundary-spanning positions forces employees to balance productivity with quality. This challenges everyone in these roles to deliver consistent high-quality service and makes management of boundary-spanning positions much more difficult. Customers further complicate the mix, as their participation in the delivery of a service also has the potential to negatively affect their own satisfaction and the satisfaction of others. This is especially true if customers fail to understand their role in or responsibilities for the service transaction. In an academic library environment, for example, this is often witnessed when undergraduate students arrive with a research assignment and ask where the history books are. The consultant must engage the student with protracted questioning to elicit what area of history the student is studying. Meanwhile, the graduate student waiting behind the undergraduate with a quick question physically displays his dissatisfaction with the undergraduate's "ignorance" and the consultant's "coddling" of the ignorant undergraduate. He is seething, making scowling faces, and shifting from one foot to the other. The graduate student's discomfort is affecting others waiting for assistance and distracting the consultant working with the undergraduate. In this example, everyone contributes to the service gap.

Boundary-spanning positions also require the provision of emotional labor. This further influences the performance gap as library and information consultants must smile and display verbal and physical welcoming behaviors, even when they don't feel like smiling, offering a warm greeting, or closing a transaction politely after dealing with an impolite, unreasonable customer. Failure to display appropriate emotions may detrimentally affect customers' perceptions of their service experience. When employees are required to display emotions they do not feel, the reality is that significant stress results. Therefore to maximize consultant effectiveness and minimize the organization's failure to meet service designs and standards, careful attention must be given when developing employee recruitment and retention strategies. Such strategies must attract and retain individuals capable of handling emotional labor and the stress a library and information consultant job can generate. Further, managers of library and information consultants must structure a consultant's responsibilities to balance onstage activities with backstage downtime. Time away from the public gives library and information consultants the opportunity to recover and cope with stress and frustration. Further, repeated coaching and training on communication techniques, conflict resolution, or problem-solving skills are also needed to help mitigate some problems. A supportive work environment or Service-Scape that addresses employees' physical and emotional needs may also help.

Like customers, employees thrive on quality service. Positive interactions with consumers should satisfy the library and information consultant and leave him craving more of the same activity. While this is the ideal, however, not every individual will succeed in a library and information consultant role. As noted in chapter 1, some skills and talents for interacting with the public are innate and cannot be modeled or taught. Thus, when libraries recruit and screen individuals to serve as library and information consultants, they must consider the candidate's energy and interpersonal skills. They must question whether the individual will be able to effectively market or sell the library's services and resources. They must consider her knowledge of libraries, including their culture and structure, and the information resources contained both within the library itself and outside at large. In the public library setting, they must ask whether the consultant would be able to adjust her interactions to the customer's level of education or understanding. The candidate's co–production abilities must also be considered. In an academic library, would the candidate be able to coach a student through a difficult assignment using the library's special collections?

Further, the interviewing library must consider whether the library and information consultant personally embodies the five dimensions of service quality: reliability, responsiveness, assurance, empathy, and tangibles.[3] Will the candidate inspire consumer trust, giving a consumer confidence that all of his questions are valued and appreciated? Does the candidate present herself in a way that attracts or repels potential clients? Will consumers perceive this individual as responsive to their needs? Can this consultant deliver the service promised to the consumer? Does the candidate possess the right skills and competencies? Does this individual have an inclination for service? Does her personality naturally exhibit compassion, helpfulness, or sociability?[4]

Figure 4.1 offers a sample job posting for a library and information consultant operating in an academic library. Note the emphasis on accountability and proactive behaviors. The successful candidate not only must be able to develop relationships with library customers, but have the skills to take a disciplined and structured approach to finding and maintaining these customer relationships. He must also be able to identify or assist with crafting objective measures of success so that he can communicate both his value and the value of the library organization to potential customer groups. A successful library and information consultant cannot be risk-adverse. He must be willing to try new programs and services, experience failure, and regroup to try another solution when necessary. Any position description or job posting for a library and information consultant must reflect the needs of the library organization and the community it serves. Its premise,

Figure 4.1

SAMPLE POSITION POSTING:

Library and Information Consultant

Orchard Park University seeks a Library and Information Consultant to interact with students and faculty out of its Clifford T. Roland Library. The successful candidate will possess in-depth knowledge of and functional expertise with library and information resources and

- demonstrate ability to increase usage of library services and information resources
- demonstrate ability to build, maintain, and grow relationships with library customers
- proactively seek opportunities to develop and implement library services and programs that contribute to student and faculty success
- educate and enable consumers to execute information searches and evaluate the quality of resources discovered
- articulate and develop persuasive and actionable recommendations for incorporating library and information resources into academic coursework
- actively identify, measure, and analyze consumer student and faculty information needs and priorities
- assist with the identification of objectives and success metrics
- actively participate in planning, coordination, execution, training; and ongoing support of new services
- encourage informed risk-taking; stimulate innovation by offering creative solutions to problems and identifying and developing service opportunities
- actively lead and/or participate in quality improvement initiatives

REQUIRED QUALIFICATIONS:
MLS or equivalent graduate degree; three or more years of experience working in public services in a library environment; must possess a passion for libraries and information and demonstrate drive and initiative; ability to adapt to independent and team-oriented environment; excellent verbal and written communication skills, including ability to articulate viewpoint and negotiate; positive attitude; ability to manage conflict and change effectively; flexibility in accomplishing objectives; strong analytical, troubleshooting, and problem resolution skills; ability to pay attention to detail and quality standards.

PREFERRED QUALIFICATIONS:
Knowledge of or certification in Lean, Six Sigma, or another quality management discipline; documented track record of success as a project manager; experience in an academic library.

however, should be focused on results, helping customers define their needs and acquire the skills and competencies to address these needs and asking consultants to develop services, action plans, and other initiatives to meet these needs.

While hiring the right people to serve as library and information consultants requires careful selection during the interview and screening process, a concentrated effort on the part of the library organization to compete for the best people is also necessary. Compensation and benefits alone will not attract and retain talented library and information consultants. Investment in employees will—along with careful design of job responsibilities, training, and empowerment practices. Managers of the library and information consultant will be required to make many trade-offs between cost-effectiveness, service quality, and productivity. By empowering consultants to customize service offerings for consumers and make real-time decisions, for example, managers may facilitate faster response time and enable consultants to provide less bureaucratic service. This same customization, however, may also result in slower, inconsistent service delivery. A customer may perceive she has been treated unfairly when an individual in front of her received a detailed response from one employee, while she received a short response to a different question from another. The quality and consistency of the library and information consultant's service product may suffer if managers fail to provide well-defined service parameters, training, and controls for empowerment. Further, empowerment is not appropriate for all employees or situations. Developing a mutual understanding between managers and consultants regarding the scope of empowerment, although a significant challenge, is necessary to balance customer needs and satisfaction. Thus consultants and managers must work together to collect, analyze, share, and act on information about organizational performance. If employees understand how elements of their performance directly influence operational efficiencies and effectiveness, and are given appropriate rewards for enhancing operational efficiencies and effectiveness, they may better succeed at providing exceptional service for their customers at their customers' point of need. Empowered employees also have the potential to create lasting relationships with customers, promoting a cycle of success and satisfaction, as well as developing loyal customers.

Managing Consultant Supply with Customer Demand

Another major challenge for any manager responsible for a team of library and information consultants is to match consultant availability with customer demand. Some finesse is required; as in any service industry, financial, physical, and time restraints all influence an organization's success with balancing capacity and maximizing customer satisfaction. When consumer demand fails to meet capacity, for instance, productivity is compromised. Consultants stand around with no work to do. This negatively affects the organization's labor costs. Conversely, excess demand often results in lost customers, especially as overburdened staff loses the ability to deliver services as promised. In such situations, as customers waste time waiting in line, their frustration rises. Some will lose faith in the organization, especially if they are turned away without receiving service. Others may experience disgust while facilities suffer. During exam periods in an academic library, for example, overcrowding and increased noise will repel an individual seeking a quiet place to study. As cleaning crews cannot attend to library restrooms or other public spaces quickly enough during these periods to keep up with customer use, additional consumers will seek alternative working venues, perhaps permanently. The ideal is to balance all forms of organizational capacity with consumer demand.

Managing fluctuating demand for library and information consultants' services requires a detailed understanding of various market segments. Demand for consultants' services in an academic library may be clearly mapped to various times during the academic school year. While faculty's and graduate students' need for assistance with research projects may be ongoing, undergraduates' needs can be predicted from week to week. To disambiguate random versus nonrandom patterns of undergraduate demand, models may be constructed, using techniques such as exponential smoothing to inform staff deployment.[5] An exponential smoothing model allows the consultant to input factors such as the number of consumers approaching an information desk each day in relation to the day of the week and the week of the semester, and then use this information to accurately forecast the number of consumers who may approach the information desk at the same time the following semester or year. Knowing that more consultant services are needed during the third, sixth, twelfth, and final week of a semester, for instance, will inform planning.

Most often, it is not appropriate for a manager of library and information consultants to add labor capacity to address fluctuations in customer demand. The knowledge and skills required to successfully function as a library and information consultant mean that it is not realistic to hire part-time, seasonable employees to address increased demand for services. Thus managers must either cross-train employees from other library departments or develop strategies for shifting customer demand to meet capacity. Such strategies include developing and communicating incentives for students that encourage them to make an appointment with library and information consultants during quieter times during the semester. A transparent online calendar system, similar to online reservation systems used by small hotels that display what dates and times are already booked, may be helpful. Adjustment of service hours may also be appropriate. If library and information consultants do not provide service on Sunday afternoons, this practice may be reconsidered during periods of high demand. An integrated marketing communications plan that carefully explains the optimal time to work with a library and information consultant for maximizing student success, or reasons to work with the consultant during off-peak times, may also be developed and executed.

Regardless, while fluctuations in consumer demand and consultant capacity must be managed, some waits will be inevitable. The time it takes to assist one customer with a straightforward question of fact will be significantly less than the time required to assist another customer with translating an abstract concept into a workable search strategy. To maintain relationships, however, customer waits must be managed or the customer will seek an alternative. Although waits themselves do not affect customer satisfaction, the experience of the wait will.[6] While a customer will wait for a valuable service, for example, waiting alone will lead to more dissatisfaction than waiting with a group, as groups provide opportunities for conversation and other distractions. Thus attempts to segment individuals with similar interests in the same line may prove beneficial.

Waits that customers perceive to be unfair will be more excruciatingly felt than those considered just. Waiting for a customer to finish an in-depth interview with a library and information consultant, for example, may be exceptionally difficult for an individual with a quick question. Consumer anxiety paired with uncertainty regarding the wait time, and a lack of explanation or understanding of the reasons for the wait, also tax consumer patience and satisfaction. This is why automated call center software for many companies today thanks each individual for his call, indicates the approximate time he must wait to speak to a customer service representative, and then gives the customer the option to continue to hold or leave a telephone number at which he may be reached. Further, unoccupied customers will feel a wait more strongly than those who have been given something to do, like complete a form that will aid the library and information consultant in better understanding the consumer's research topic.

Library and information consultants can use a number of models and techniques to address waits. Selection of an appropriate queuing system especially may help to mitigate consumer anxieties. The single queue often used in bank lobbies and airport departure terminals, for instance, helps to communicate fairness, as the first-come, first-served principle is applied to all individuals in the line. This system addresses the frustration a customer experiences when facing a multiple queue system if the customer perceives he chose the wrong line to wait in. This experience intensifies as individuals in parallel lines complete their transactions while the customer continues to wait for a consultant to finish working with the individual preceding him. Alternatively, a number system, where arriving individuals take a number to hold their position in line, may also communicate fairness by preserving the first-come, first-served principle. With this model and the single queue, however, the consumer may not be able to choose his service provider. Understanding queuing models may assist the library and information consultant with choosing the most appropriate queuing system for her real-time services. It may also aid the consultant with establishing triage and creating and tracking metrics for service quality improvement.

If a library and information consultant understands that one segment of her customer group mainly requires straightforward assistance with locating factual information, for example, she can establish systems for differentiating waiting customers. Customers with complex questions may be referred to a quiet service point, designed for more in-depth consultation. This frees the consultant working at a main service point to focus on the needs of her market specialization. Another option would be for the library and information consultants to implement a paging system, similar to those seen in mid-scale restaurants, where a greeter records individuals' names on arrival and hands each a pager so that they may entertain themselves elsewhere in the building or work on other activities while the consultant is finishing up with the consumer ahead of the individual in line. Both examples listed here have risks. The first assumes that the consumer will be able to locate the consultant group he had been referred to. The risk of a dropped referral is a significant reality. Calling ahead or asking the consultant to either escort the referred client to the next service point or meet the client at a predetermined location may mitigate such a risk. The second relies on the consumer to self-entertain. If the consumer cannot identify other activities to occupy his time, or is uncertain regarding the time it will take for the consultant to become available, he may abandon the line, fearing he's been forgotten.

Of course all of this assumes the library and information consultant is working from a defined service point. This may not always be appropriate or optimal. To best serve the customer, in some instances, the library and information consultant must be colocated with the consumer. Embedding a librarian in an academic department, for instance, may better meet researchers' needs at their point of need. Further, a reservation system can be established, especially if consultants are able to work out of offices. Reservation systems can effectively smooth demand, promising customers that a consultant will be available at a prearranged time and place. Such a system may be effective in encouraging consumers to interact with the consultant at an off-peak time. A trade-off must be made when implementing such a system, however, as added costs result from unfilled appointment times, or instances where consumers make an appointment just in case but fail to show up.

Managing Financial and Capital Resources Using Impact Evaluation

Finally, as stewards of the resources given to them both by public or private sources, library and information consultants must strategically allocate their financial and capital resources to demonstrate the value of their services and efficiently and effectively serve their client populations. It is not enough to just manage cash flows and expenses. Resources must be aligned with the programs that most effectively serve the populations the library organization wishes to target. Although businesses traditionally use profit (defined as revenue minus costs) to measure the success of a product or program, library and information consultants, by the nature of their work, must expand their thinking to include other criteria. The success of a library and information consultant's service product is affected by the allocation of financial and capital resources. Focus must remain on maximizing customer value and both demonstrating and communicating the impact of the consultant's professional services.

Demonstration of impact is broader than regular assessment or evaluative programs. Impact distinguishes itself by focusing on how a service, product, or program has affected people's lives. Library and information consultants must determine whether their service or services changed an individual's behavior or way of thinking about a problem. They must question whether the consumer's knowledge of the information resources relevant to his subject interest increased as a result of the consultant's service product. They must determine whether their services made a measurable difference in the consumer's life. Too often library administrators rely on outputs or counts to communicate the effectiveness of a library service or program. Measures such as gate-count, circulation volume, and website visits, however, have little to no actionable meaning, especially if consumers visit the library to access a coffee bar located behind the gate on the first floor.

Quality impact evaluations are structured around clear programmatic objectives and intended program outcomes. Objectives must be time-limited in scope and linked to an organization's mission and or vision. Objectives focus the consultant's and the organization's practical application of human, financial, and capital resources by translating a mission or vision into an overall goal the organization wishes to achieve. Outcomes are linked to objectives and represent the changes in knowledge, affect or behavior, skills, and attitudes that can directly be attributed to a service or program. Programs often have intended and unintended outcomes or consequences. The discipline of crafting intended measurable outcomes in writing, however, forces the consultant to determine how she will know whether the program made a difference in people's lives.

Grant applicants are often required to include plans for outcomes-based evaluation in their program proposals. The United States Institute of Museum and Library Services (IMLS), specifically, provides training on outcomes-based planning and evaluation for grant applicants on its website.[7] Designed to assist applicants with planning, constructing, and evaluating IMLS-funded projects, the online "Shaping Outcomes: Making a Difference in Libraries and Museums" instruction is a valuable tool for getting started.[8] Many land-grant universities with active extension programs also provide detailed documentation and training for designing outcomes-based evaluation programs. The University of Wisconsin's Cooperative Extension program, for instance, provides instructions, templates, examples, and other materials for constructing logic models, a useful tool for individuals who are both planning and designing programs or services.[9]

Logic models illustrate the relationships between a target population's situation or needs, the inputs in which the program staff will invest to change people's lives, the outputs and activities of the program, and the program's intended outcomes. The logic model may also display the assumptions and external factors that drive or influence the program. There is no right or wrong way to construct a logic model. Used in concert with the tools already covered in this book, the logic model can assist the consultant working to design service products with impact, and aid this individual or the library in allocating human and financial resources to this and other service products.

Figure 4.2 provides one example of a logic model for a library and information consultant working with a local art museum to develop needs-based community programming. Note that this model broadly articulates the human and financial resources required to implement the program. The audience the program is intended for is listed. Further, measurable short-, medium-, and long-term outcomes are identified. This particular model doesn't visually represent the situation or needs analysis, assumptions, or external factors influencing the program. These factors may be referenced elsewhere in other documents, or outlined in a separate project narrative.

Summary

To function as consummate professionals, library and information consultants must address gaps 3 and 4 of the Integrated Gaps Model of Service Quality: failure to meet service designs and standards and failure to deliver a service as promised. By understanding and managing their roles in service

Figure 4.2

Logic Model for Joint Library/Museum Program

	OUTPUTS			OUTCOMES/IMPACT	
INPUTS	ACTIVITIES	PARTICIPATION	SHORT TERM	MEDIUM TERM	LONG TERM
■ Funding and staff to program and lead community forums for discourse and dialogue ■ Partnership to develop educator curriculum ■ Funding and staff to provide community outreach programming	■ Website ■ Repository of discourse ■ Interactive community ■ Exhibition ■ Trading cards and other educational print materials which support online and live programming activities ■ Digitized collections ■ Curriculum	■ Educators, grades 6–8 and 9–12 ■ Middle school and high school students ■ Intergenerational (seniors and youth) ■ Community partners	Participants will ■ Engage in immediate discourse and dialogue in library and museum forums ■ Express opinions; share reaction to art and social issues ■ Indicate interest in participating in program activities ■ Create artifacts ■ Contribute written, recorded, and visual materials to the program website	Participants will ■ Understand the role the artist plays in directing public attention toward important social issues (knowledge) ■ Recognize younger and older generations as a source of information and cultural perspectives (attitude) ■ Appreciate and respect younger and older generations as a source of information and cultural perspectives (affect)	Participants will ■ Engage in ongoing discourse around social issues ■ Participate in social issues regularly ■ Use the library and museum as sources of community knowledge

delivery, library and information consultants are better positioned to deliver quality service products as promised to their customers. They are also better able to minimize their performance gaps. Addressing gaps 3 and 4 requires dedicated, conscious management of human resources and the inherent challenges faced by individuals operating in boundary-spanning positions. Hiring, retention, development, and empowerment decisions must reflect this reality. Identifying individuals with both service inclination and service competence is imperative when filling open library and information consultant positions. Further, managers of library and information consultants must provide well-defined service parameters, training, and controls to empower consultants to develop lasting relationships with customers.

Strategies to manage consultant availability and customer demand are also necessary. Knowledge of queuing models, the psychology of waiting, and techniques for smoothing customer demand with consultant supply all contribute to minimizing performance gaps. By choosing a specific queuing model when designing a service, a consultant can address the benefits and limitations of the queue and structure the service offering accordingly.

Lastly, by understanding the impact of a library and information consultant's programs and services, the consultant and library organization are better positioned to strategically allocate their financial and capital resources. Quality impact evaluations require that program objectives and outcomes be clearly committed in writing. Such discipline forces the consultant to plan how she will determine whether a service product or program effectively affected change in an individual or community's knowledge, behavior, attitudes, or skills. Logic models may visually assist with the development and communication of a program's objectives and outcomes.

Notes

1. A. Parasuraman, Valarie A. Zeithaml, and Leonard L. Berry, "A Conceptual Model of Service Quality and Its Implications for Future Research," *Journal of Marketing* 49, no. 4 (1985): 41–50.
2. Christopher H. Lovelock and Jochen Wirtz, *Services Marketing: People, Technology, Strategy,* 7th ed. (Boston: Prentice Hall, 2011).
3. Valarie A. Zeithaml, Mary Jo Bitner, and Dwayne D. Gremler, *Services Marketing: Integrating Customer Focus across the Firm,* 4th ed., (Boston: McGraw-Hill/Irwin, 2006), 358.
4. Ibid., 368.

5. Mohammad Ahmadi, Parthasarati Dileepan, Sarla R. Murgai, and Wendy Roth, "An Exponential Smoothing Model for Predicting Traffic in the Library and at the Reference Desk," *Bottom Line: Managing Library Finances* 21, no. 2 (2008): 37–48.

6. David H. Maister, "The Psychology of Waiting Lines," in *The Service Encounter: Managing Employee/Customer Interaction in Service Businesses,* ed. John A. Czepiel, Michael R. Solomon, and Carol F. Suprenant (Lexington, MA: Lexington Books, 1985), 113–23.

7. Institute of Museum and Library Services, "Outcome Based Evaluation," http://imls .gov/applicants/obe.shtm.

8. Institute of Museum and Library Services and Indiana University-Purdue University Indianapolis, "Shaping Outcomes: Making a Difference in Libraries and Museums," www.shapingoutcomes.org/about.htm.

9. University of Wisconsin Cooperative Extension, "Logic Model," www.uwex.edu/ces/ pdande/evaluation/evallogicmodel.html.

Developing the Infrastructure and Culture for Continuous Quality Improvement

ll consultants embody their service product and must deliver quality results in order to attract and maintain a customer base. Quality functions as a product differentiator, leading a consumer to choose a library and information consultant's services over a search engine or bookstore. When consultants operate independently, they alone are responsible for the quality of their relationship with their clients and the quality of their service product. In a library organization, where multiple individuals may function as library and information consultants, a more methodical effort is required to assure quality delivery of service. This is especially important, as failure to consciously monitor and improve quality leads to many kinds of waste.

This chapter focuses on the development and maintenance of an infrastructure for continuously improving the library and information consultant's service product. It begins by reviewing the costs of quality, highlighting the unseen consequences that result when a service or product fails to address customer needs. It continues with an introduction to three proven quality improvement disciplines or frameworks that have been successfully implemented by libraries and organizations throughout the world: Lean, Six Sigma, and the Malcolm Baldrige Quality Award. By utilizing the philosophies, structure, and tools of these programs, a library organization can ensure their library and information consultants are delivering the service product promised to their customers.

Examining the Costs of Quality

Services invite variability, and consumers and consultants both influence the quality of the final service product by providing the inputs and outputs necessary for the service provision. There are significant consequences for both the consumer and the library and information consultant when a quality service product is not delivered. These consequences are not just financial in nature, but may permanently affect customer relationships, compromise efficiency, or cause unnecessary employee distress.

The quality improvement disciplines recognize that successful delivery of quality products is not limited to identifying and removing defective goods from circulation before they reach customers.[1] Investment that prevents defective or poor quality goods from occurring in the first place is also required. Experts divide the costs of quality into two components: the costs of conformance or good quality, and the costs of nonconformance or poor quality. Ideally the costs of good quality and poor quality occur before the product reaches the customer and eliminate a potentially dissatisfied customer. The total costs required to provide a near-perfect product to the customer represent the overall cost of quality.

The aim of most quality improvement disciplines is to reduce the overall cost of quality by lowering the cost of good quality. Good quality requires activities involving prevention and appraisal that occur before the actual delivery of the product or service. By building quality into the actual product, process, or service, the consultant or organization can minimize or eliminate failure costs and benchmark for continuous quality improvement. Prevention costs include both the human and financial investments required for quality planning, product testing, vendor evaluation, employee training, data collection, and quality improvement projects. These costs are incurred prior to production with the goals of reducing process variation and eliminating waste. Appraisal costs include various types of product inspection, and are intended to identify problems before the product reaches the consumer. These costs may be much more difficult for the library and information consultant to manage, due to the real-time nature of their service product. A few ill-chosen words, for example, can prematurely end an interview structured to elicit the consumer's information need, especially if the consumer perceived the consultant failing to take his query seriously. A simple question such as "Where are you from?" may be interpreted as a denial of service by an individual from an underrepresented minority group, even though the consultant's intention was to help determine a consumer's library borrowing and database access privileges. Such an innocent question cannot be taken back if it is readily apparent the consumer received a negative message from the exchange. Since inspection of a verbal answer before delivery is nearly impossible, prevention costs such as cultural sensitivity education may prove more useful for a library and information consultant.

Poor quality results when products fail to conform to product specifications or standards. The ultimate cost of poor quality is a dissatisfied customer, who is ready to bemoan the substandard quality of the consultant's product, process, or service to anyone who will listen. Poor quality products require both financial and human resources to address. Costs include the resources required to resolve complaints, rework faulty products, address delays, recover lost sales, redesign a defective product, or scrap a defective product that cannot be fixed. Poor quality is usually revealed after the consumer receives the product or service, requiring the consultant to incur internal and external failure costs. In the manufacturing sector, for example, a crib recall represents an external failure cost. The manufacturer must reimburse the consumer for his purchase or provide the parts and labor for a warranty repair. The time a manufacturer or service organization spends to receive and resolve complaints is an additional cost. Further, by releasing a defective, poor quality product, the organization risks permanently losing a customer, especially if a competitor offers a similar product.

Internal failure costs include the costs for scrapping or reworking a defective product, delays, and shortages. In a library organization, these costs may be incurred following a failed database launch. Specifically, if an academic library chooses an alternative specialty database in an effort to conserve financial resources, and the chosen database fails to index journals in a subdiscipline in which the university has strategically chosen to invest, internal failure costs will occur while the library repurchases, relicenses, and recatalogs the cancelled database to address customer dissatisfaction.

Numerous studies prove that strategic investment in quality does dramatically increase an organization's profitability by efficiently and effectively utilizing an organization's human, capital, and financial resources.[2] Additional benefits include competitive advantage and market share gain, as well as improvement in employee relations, fact-based decision making, and customer focus. The costs saved by overcoming the "engagement gap," defined as "the lack of strong feelings of ownership and enthusiasm for improvement by people who do the work every day," are also significant.[3] By actively involving employees in improvement projects, organizations draw on a valuable resource for identifying consumer needs and desires and questioning accepted practices in effort to eliminate waste.

Establishing the Quality Infrastructure: Lean, Six Sigma, and the Baldrige National Quality Program

Library and information consultants can choose from a number of quality improvement tools celebrated by management experts over the past century. Elements of each have significant merit, especially for specific projects. A tool alone, however, is not nearly as powerful as the quality improvement disciplines of Lean, Six Sigma, and the Baldrige National Quality Program. To achieve performance excellence through continuous improvement, organizations must systematically, strategically, and deliberately assess, monitor, and address the quality of their entire service portfolio. Such discipline is required from the library and information consultant to both attract and retain clients. Although a quality improvement initiative should be initiated and supported by top management of a library organization, if no such quality improvement program exists, consultants can model their own program for performance excellence based on one of these disciplines. By consciously talking about quality, through disciplined measurement and follow-up, consultants can significantly improve response times, productivity, and the overall customer experience. Such practice illustrates where and how consultants must change and adjust their practice to better address customer needs.

Lean

Often referred to as "Lean Manufacturing" or "Lean Production," Lean represents a quality improvement philosophy focused on reducing and eliminating waste by optimizing flow. Developed by Toyota in the mid-1980s,

Lean works to remove non-value added work by addressing the seven *muda* or wastes.[4] These wastes, with examples pertinent to the library sector, include:

- *Defects,* or the time required to physically inspect and address defects. In libraries this often occurs in catalog maintenance. Failure to properly withdraw a book, for example, leads to confusion when catalog entries indicate the library owns a copy, but patrons and staff are unable to find the item on the shelf.
- *Overproduction,* or the costs that result when an organization produces more than customers demand. This occurs when libraries purchase multiple copies of a book anticipating high circulation, which is never realized.
- *Transportation,* or unnecessarily moving the product. When a consumer is required to move from an information desk to an office that a library and information consultant has designated for more in-depth consultations, a transportation waste occurs.
- *Waiting,* or the time that is wasted while a good is not being transported or processed. In academic libraries this often occurs when materials wait months or even years in cataloging, waiting until staff is available to process them.
- *Inventory,* or the waste incurred while finished goods sit in storage, waiting to be sold, or raw materials sit on a receiving dock, waiting to be processed. In libraries this waste occurs any time a book sits behind a circulation desk, waiting to be reshelved.
- *Motion,* or the time lost when people or equipment must be moved to finish processing product. When library employees start processing an interlibrary loan request on one computer workstation, and then have to move to another to scan the request, a waste of motion occurs.
- *Processing,* or providing more features or services than the customer requires. In the library setting this occurs when a library and information consultant provides more detail than the consumer required when answering a question. Library catalogs also frequently provide more granular detail than needed by the average consumer.

Some quality improvement experts add an additional waste not indentified by Lean: the waste of the lost customer. This is often considered the most unnecessary and egregious waste of all. When organizations fail to deliver quality services and products, they risk losing established customers who once passionately used and advocated the organization's brand to others. While new customers require significant investment to attract, established customers do not. Established customers are more likely to repeatedly purchase and utilize an organization's services. Further, established customers require less training, as they already understand the value of the library and information consultant's service product. This means the established customer ultimately costs less to serve. Thus, maintaining the established customer is a valuable long-term strategy for any library and information consultant or organization.

Lean quality initiatives are usually organized around teams. Team members are led by a more experienced *sensei,* or teacher, who coaches team members to seize a crisis or create opportunities to improve a process. The role of leadership is extremely important in a Lean organization, as Lean is both an initiative and a culture. Leadership sets the vision for the organization's Lean initiative and must communicate this vision and their objectives to their employees. Team members identify and select improvement projects that are in line with leadership's vision and objectives. Using the tools identified below with other techniques, the team studies the current state of the process and then collectively works to achieve flow by brainstorming, studying, piloting, and implementing alternatives.

By focusing on improving processes by removing waste, Lean can reduce the time to complete each activity in a process, and thus minimize costs. The discipline relies heavily on value-stream mapping to identify each stage of a process. When constructing a value-stream map, the consultant starts with the customer and works backward to the raw materials or inputs necessary to create the product. The information flows required to complete a process are identified on the map, along with the time it takes to complete each stage of the process (value-added time), the time it takes to complete each stage of the process, and the idle times between stages in the process (non-value-added time). The process of creating a value-stream map can assist library and information consultants with visualizing their processes, provide a common language for discussing these processes, and provide a baseline from which to measure the success of implemented improvements. The goal of value-stream mapping is to identify opportunities to reduce the overall process lead time and better align it with customer demand.

Figure 5.1 provides a value-stream map for a library's e-mail consultation service. Starting with the output "Customer Receives Answer," each stage of the process for answering questions was identified, starting at the right and moving toward the left. Stages are represented with process boxes, and within each process box, circles indicate the number of employees required for that particular stage of the process. Thus, after the assistant assigned questions, the map shows that up to four consultants answered these questions at any given time. Work-in-progress inventory is represented by the triangles. This map indicates that between the time the consultants pulled the questions to process at eleven o'clock on Tuesday and began to research answers, there were twenty-four questions in inventory. Cycle time is indicated by the letters C/T and represents the average time it takes to complete one stage of the process for each question. This means if there were twenty-four questions submitted at nine o'clock at night, it took the assistant an average of three minutes to initially read each question individually, and an additional minute to assign each question to the appropriate consultant.

For each shift, the total number of minutes available was listed beneath the cycle time. Since the consultants and assistant work Monday through Friday from eight to five and take a one-hour break for lunch, there were 480 minutes available to process customer questions each day. Lastly, the value-added time versus the non-value-added time required to process each question was indicated by the high and low lines on the bottom of the map. Note that three hours of non-value-added time occurred while the questions sat in inventory, waiting for the consultants to pull them from the queue at eleven o'clock on Tuesday.

On average it took the assistant and consultants operating the e-mail consultation service a total of twenty-two minutes to research, answer, and send an answer to one customer's question. The total lead time from when the customer submitted his question to when he received an answer, however, was actually fourteen hours and twenty-two minutes. If, after constructing this map, a library and information consultant determined that this lead time was unacceptable, he could assign additional assistants to pull, read, and assign questions. He could also increase the number of consultants

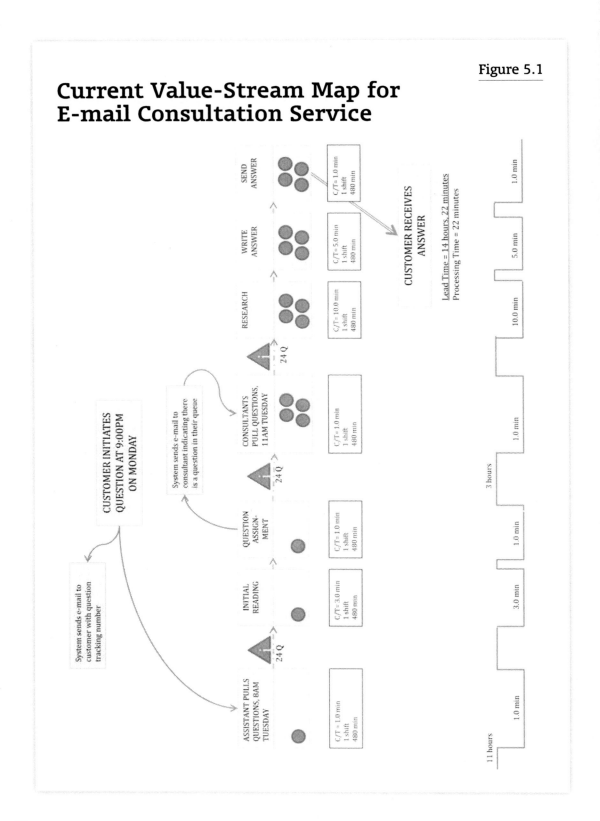

Current Value-Stream Map for E-mail Consultation Service

Figure 5.1

available to answer questions, or extend the hours of consultant availability. The library and information consultant could also decide to empower the assistant to answer a number of questions, without having to assign them to another consultant first.

Other Lean tools include *takt time,* a measurement that divides the total available hours to create a product divided by the rate at which customers demand the product. The ideal is to balance takt time. Using takt time, the library and information consultant can benchmark efforts to optimally staff services in line with customer demand. Lean also heavily relies on the Ishikawa (Cause-and-Effect) diagram to provide a qualitative means to identify the root cause of a problem. Also known as a fishbone diagram, the Ishikawa diagram encourages consultants to categorize the potential causes of a defect or an event into six groups: people, methods, machines, materials, measurements, and environment. Figure 5.2 illustrates the potential causes for failing to record directional or reference questions at a circulation desk in a library's Libstats database. Note that the problem event or defect is written on the horizontal line or "spine" of the fish. The potential causes were then grouped into the appropriate Ishikawa categories on the diagonal lines and further broken down in detail. Also note that not all of the categories were included. Further, some potential causes were applicable to more than one category. Through the process of creating the Ishikawa diagram, the hope is that the true cause, or likely potential cause of the problem, will become readily apparent. The team constructing the diagram can then examine each of the likely potential causes in detail, in an effort to find and correct the root cause of the problem.

Lean also advocates *poka yoke,* a concept focused on using visual or other signals to either error-proof a process or capture a human operator's attention when an error is occurring. In the library environment, this is already implemented with discovery systems such as OCLC's WorldCat, which can pre-populate data for users' ILLiad Interlibrary Loan request forms online and allow libraries to offer unmediated ILL requests to their users. Such systems save processing time and eliminate processing errors. For a library and information consultant, a checklist for handling information requests from certain customers may also serve as a mechanism to *poka yoke* a service process.

Figure 5.2

Ishikawa Diagram

Examining Potential Causes for Not Recording Directional/Reference
Questions Asked at the Circulation Desk in Libstats Database

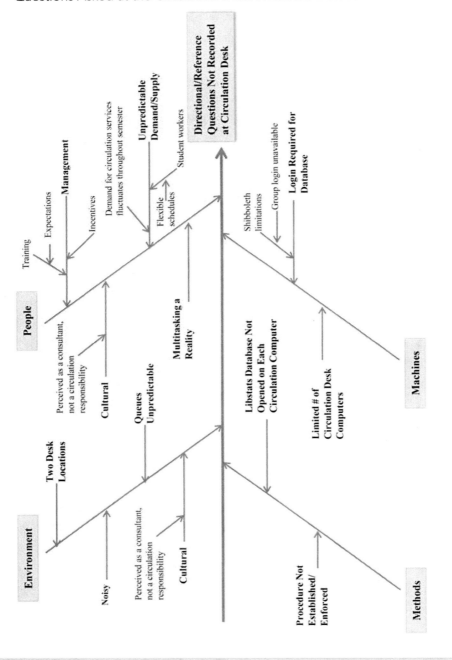

Six Sigma

Often used in association with Lean (i.e., Lean Six Sigma), Six Sigma focuses on minimizing variation by bringing a process under statistical control.[5] Like Lean, Six Sigma is project-based, and heavily reliant on a number of quality tools. The discipline emphasizes the removal of process defects, errors, and inefficiencies to achieve improvements in customer satisfaction, cost, quality, process speed, and invested capital. Like Lean, Six Sigma quality initiatives also rely on teams and are implemented throughout an organization. Unlike Lean, however, a Six Sigma initiative is hierarchically structured, with project teams led by a Six Sigma Black Belt whose role is to coach and advise a team on the Six Sigma philosophy and tools and assist the team with executing a project. An organization's Six Sigma initiative consists of Project Champions, followed by Master Black Belts, Black Belts, Green Belts, and project team members. Project Champions either take direction from the senior leadership of the organization or serve on the senior leadership team for the organization. These individuals set the vision for the organization's Six Sigma implementation and work with the Master Black Belts to identify, select, and prioritize strategic Six Sigma projects. They are also responsible for empowering the project teams and providing the financial and human resources required to complete a project.

Master Black Belts train and mentor the Black Belts. Their primary role is to support Six Sigma projects throughout the organization, serving as the resident Six Sigma experts. Master Black Belts have successfully completed a number of Six Sigma projects on their own and received the highest level of training. They are responsible for translating the Six Sigma philosophy and making sure Black Belts ask the appropriate questions and apply the optimal quality tools to a project. Black Belts lead individual Six Sigma projects and coach and train Green Belts. Green Belts serve on project teams, assisting the Black Belts with project execution. This service, however, is in addition to the Green Belt's other regular duties. Anyone else who participates on a project is considered a regular project team member.

Six Sigma projects are organized using the Define-Measure-Analyze-Improve-Control (DMAIC) methodology. During the Define phase, team members draft a project charter to clarify the process to be examined, identify project stakeholders, articulate project objectives and deliverables, identify desired outcomes, and create a project timeline. A key task of the Define phase is to represent a process in terms of the mathematical function $Y = f(x)$, where (x) represents the input variable(s) for the process and Y represents the process output or outcome. A team of library and information consultants working on a project to improve their telephone consultation services, therefore, might identify (x) as their call center software and staff, and Y as reducing the number of rings before a call is answered.

Tools which prove useful for articulating the Voice of the Customer are applied during the Define phase. This includes the Kano model, affinity diagram, and the CTQC tree. Additional tools, such as the SIPOC diagram, are helpful for identifying and communicating to team members and the organization's leadership the project's relevant suppliers, inputs, process elements, outputs, and customers. The Lean value-stream map provided for in figure 5.1 was reconceived as a SIPOC diagram for an e-mail consultation in an academic library for figure 5.3. Note that a supplier can also function as a customer. The answer represents the output on which quality is judged, and the process is represented by a flowchart. The consultant's knowledge along with the publisher's product is required to produce the output. The construction of the SIPOC diagram forces the team to work together to clarify the purpose of their project. It also identifies the project's high-level, overarching process.

The Measure phase requires the project team to measure the baseline performance of the defined process and develop a data collection plan. The purpose of the Measure phase is to gather enough information to focus the improvement effort. By gathering factual information about the process, the team can determine the source of problems contributing to the poor performance or quality. One key activity during the Measure phase is the establishment of Process Sigma Level. This represents the baseline capability of the process identified for improvement. Process Sigma Level is determined by calculating a process's Defects Per Million Opportunities (DPMO) and then locating the Process Sigma Level in a Sigma Conversion table.[6] To calculate DPMO, the consultant must first determine the number of defects present in a process and multiply this number by one million. The resulting number must then be divided by the number of defect opportunities per unit multiplied by the total number of units. Thus, if a supervisor were evaluating a library and information consultant using a checklist of twenty-four expectations for the consultant's interactions with clients, when the consultant fails

Figure 5.3

SIPOC Diagram for E-mail Consultation Service in an Academic Library

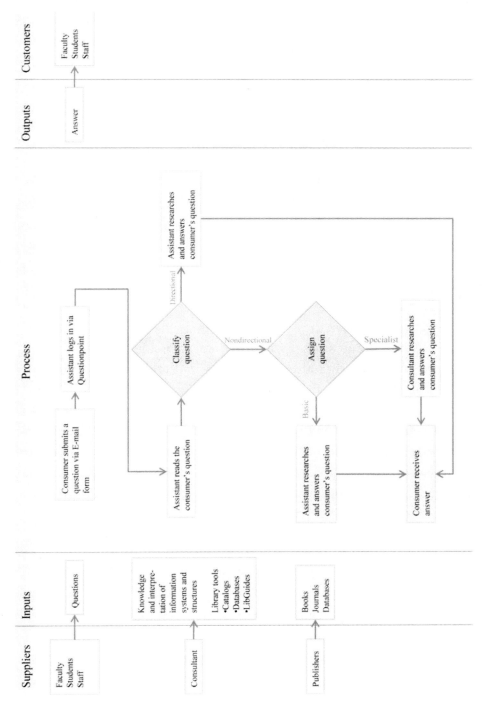

to display an expected behavior, this would be recorded as a defect. If during a one-hour observation, the supervisor observed the consultant interacting with thirty-five clients and recorded five defects total during all observations, the five defects would be multiplied by one million. The resulting five million would then be divided by the twenty-four opportunities for a defect to occur multiplied by thirty-five, or the total number of clients. DPMO for this example would be 5,952, resulting in a Process Sigma Level of 4.015. The goal of Six Sigma is to move the Process Sigma Level closer to value 6.0. This is accomplished by minimizing any variation in the process that contributes to the number of defects. Thus, Process Sigma Level must be recalculated during the Analyze and Improve phases to determine whether improvements to the process were successful.

Other tools used during the Measure phase include Pareto charts, the value-stream mapping techniques utilized by Lean, time-series graphs, frequency plots, and control charts. A Pareto chart graphically illustrates the frequency a problem occurs in descending order using bars and the cumulative percent contribution of all problems using a line. In figure 5.4 a Pareto chart illustrates the reasons (or defects) customers provided for not using a library in the past month. Note that customers indicated the library's hours as the most frequent reason they chose to not use the library. Access to computers and lack of group study space followed. Although an organization cannot always immediately address the category with the highest number of defects, addressing more than one category can often have a larger cumulative effect on correcting the quality problem. Project team members can utilize the Pareto chart along with other data to focus their attention on the categories that are likely contributing to the problem. This focuses their attention for the Analyze phase, where theories about the root cause of the problem are both developed and confirmed using brainstorming, Ishikawa diagrams, affinity diagrams, scatter plots, regression analysis, additional Pareto charts, and other tools as appropriate.

The Improve phase focuses on developing and implementing strategies to address the root cause or causes of the identified problem. The project team brainstorms changes to the problem process using many of the tools identified above. The team then pilot-tests potential solutions to determine whether changes to the input variables resulted in the desired change to the output or outcome for the process. Once an optimal solution is identified,

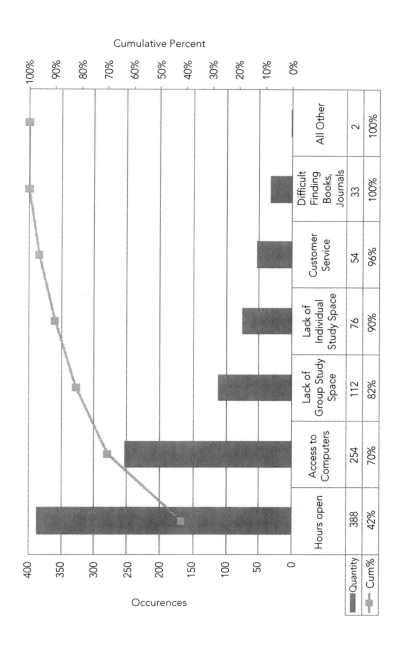

Figure 5.4

Pareto Chart Showing Customer Reasons for Not Using the Library within the Past Month

the team members draft a detailed implementation plan that includes elements such as the sequence of tasks required to implement the solution, the financial resources required, and a plan to monitor the solution. Activities such as the creation or revision of standardized operating procedures may be required during this phase. Staff may also need additional training to successfully implement the solution.

Lastly, Six Sigma recognizes that even the best solutions cannot be maintained unless action is taken to sustain the improvement over time. Activities undertaken in the Control phase are intended to ensure the process will remain stable and continue to improve over time. A written control plan identifies the data the process owner must collect regularly to continually monitor performance. The control plan positions the process owner to determine whether a problem must be addressed immediately or can be attributed to a one-time occurrence. Once the control plan is complete, the project team must effectively close the project by transferring full ownership of a process back to the process owner.

Baldrige National Quality Program

Sponsored by the U.S. Department of Commerce's National Institute of Standards and Technology (NIST), the Baldrige National Quality Program differs slightly from Lean and Six Sigma. With this program institutions seek the Malcolm Baldrige Quality Award and use the award's criteria to frame their quality improvement initiatives.[7] Most award seekers note the award itself is not as important as the institution's experience while working toward the award. To apply, institutions must document and demonstrate how they've achieved sustainable improvement in performance.

There are three categories of Baldrige Criteria for Performance Excellence available for organizations to utilize: business/nonprofits, education, and health care.[8] Figure 5.5 illustrates the structure for the seven award categories: leadership; strategic planning; customer focus; measurement, analysis, and knowledge management; workforce focus; process management; and results. Note the categories are framed by the context of the organization's profile. Each category provides detailed questions for the organization to answer. These questions assist the organization with assessing its performance and focusing improvement. The criteria also function as an organization-wide learning tool, facilitating communication and aiding the organization with focusing on the future. Many of the tools included in the overview of Lean and Six Sigma quality initiatives are also applied by institutions seeking the Baldrige Award.

Limitations of Quality Improvement Initiatives

Although Lean, Six Sigma, and the Baldrige National Quality Program all have valuable elements in common, it is important to understand the limitations of any quality improvement initiative. Most notably, each of the

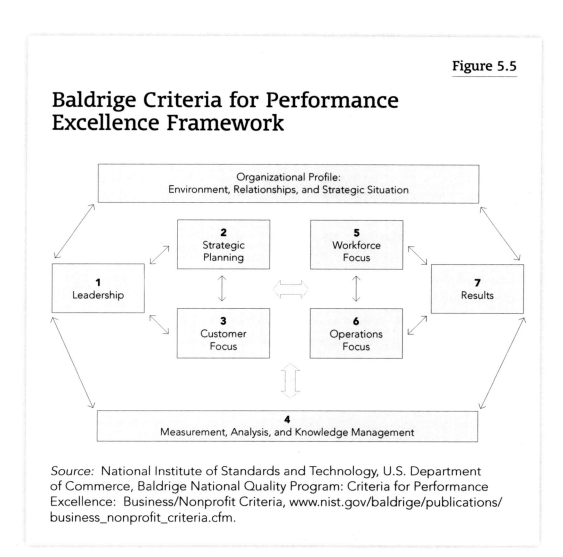

Figure 5.5

Baldrige Criteria for Performance Excellence Framework

Source: National Institute of Standards and Technology, U.S. Department of Commerce, Baldrige National Quality Program: Criteria for Performance Excellence: Business/Nonprofit Criteria, www.nist.gov/baldrige/publications/business_nonprofit_criteria.cfm.

disciplines reviewed above require a significant investment of time, personnel, and financial resources to implement. Library budgetary constraints may hinder the library and information consultant's ability to harness such a program. True organization-wide deployment of these initiatives also requires top-down administrative support, which the library and information consultant may or may not have. Further, all three disciplines rely on improving existing processes. This assumes that the existing process can be improved. If a process was fundamentally flawed when originally introduced, it may need to be rethought, discarded, or replaced. While a handful of library organizations have already successfully implemented the Baldrige National Quality Program, even fewer have experimented with Lean and Six Sigma.[9] This may benefit or challenge the library and information consultant, requiring him to seek training, wisdom, and experience for the Lean, Six Sigma, and Baldrige National Quality Program disciplines from outside of the library community.

Summary

Quality differentiates library and information consultants from their competitors. By developing and continuously improving quality service products, consultants can both attract and retain customers. This is especially important because the costs of poor quality are high. Poor quality may detrimentally and permanently affect customer relationships, institutional efficiency, and employee well-being.

There are two components driving the costs of quality: the costs of conformance and the costs of nonconformance. Most quality improvement disciplines seek to reduce the overall costs of quality through prevention and appraisal. Although building quality into the actual product, process, or service is ideal, other prevention costs such as product testing, data collection, and quality improvement projects are required. Prevention and appraisal costs should be incurred before the product reaches the consumer. Internal and external failure costs result after the consumer receives the product or service. These include the financial and human resources required to resolve complaints, manage public opinion, rework defective products, or scrap products that cannot be fixed.

By strategically investing in quality and establishing a quality infrastructure, a library organization can dramatically improve how efficiently and effectively it utilizes its human, capital, and financial resources. Disciplines such as Lean, Six Sigma, and the Baldrige National Quality Program can assist both a library organization and library and information consultants with systematically, strategically, and deliberately assessing, monitoring, and addressing the quality of their services and products. While Lean focuses on eliminating waste by optimizing flow, Six Sigma focuses on eliminating variation by bringing a process into statistical control. The Baldrige National Quality Program provides a rigorous framework of questions and documentation to encourage an organization to both assess and improve its current state of operations and processes. If system-wide organizational leadership for a quality initiative is lacking, library and information consultants may borrow concepts and tools from each of these disciplines to guide their own quality initiatives in effort to change and adjust their practice to better address customer needs.

Although most quality improvement disciplines have elements in common, they also have limitations. Lean, Six Sigma, and the Baldrige National Quality Program all focus on improving existing processes. This assumes a process already exists, or that the existing process had merit when first introduced. An organization-wide deployment of a quality improvement initiative also requires a significant investment of time, human, and financial resources. This may prove difficult to secure during a period of contracting library budgets. Few libraries have also tried to fully implement Lean, Six Sigma, or the Baldrige National Quality Program, limiting library and information consultant's ability to seek training, wisdom, and experience in deploying these quality improvement initiatives from the library community.

Notes

1. Arne Buthmann, "Cost of Quality: Not Only Failure Costs," iSixSigma, www.isix sigma.com/index.php?option=com_k2&view=item&id=937:cost-of-quality-not-only -failure-costs&Itemid=187.
2. John Ryan, "Making the Economic Case for Quality: An ASQ White Paper," American Society for Quality, www.asq.org/economic-case.
3. Ibid.

4. James P. Womack, Daniel T. Jones, and Daniel Roos, *The Machine That Changed the World: The Story of Lean Production—Toyota's Secret Weapon in the Global Car Wars That Is Revolutionizing World Industry* (New York: Free Press, 2007).

5. Peter S. Pande, Robert P. Neuman, and Roland R. Cavanagh, *The Six Sigma Way: How GE, Motorola, and Other Top Companies Are Honing Their Performance* (New York: McGraw-Hill, 2000).

6. iSixSigma, "Sigma Calculator," www.isixsigma.com/index.php?option=com_content& view=article&id=204&Itemid=392.

7. National Institute of Standards and Technology, "Baldrige National Quality Program," www.nist.gov/baldrige.

8. National Institute of Standards and Technology, "Baldrige National Quality Program: Criteria for Performance Excellence," www.nist.gov/baldrige/publications/criteria .cfm.

9. Sarah Anne Murphy, "Leveraging Lean Six Sigma to Culture, Nurture, and Sustain Assessment and Change in the Academic Library Environment," *College and Research Libraries* 70, no. 3 (2009): 215–25; Despina Dapias Wilson, Theresa Del Tufo, and Anne E. C. Norman, *The Measure of Library Excellence: Linking the Malcolm Baldrige Criteria and Balanced Scorecard Methods to Assess Service Quality* (Jefferson, NC: McFarland, 2008); Jeanne F. Voyles, Linda Dols, and Ellen Knight, "Interlibrary Loan Meets Six Sigma: The University of Arizona Library's Success Applying Process Improvement," *Journal of Interlibrary Loan, Document Delivery and Electronic Reserves* 19, no. 1 (2009): 75–94; Edward Reid-Smith, "Deriving Library Value through SWOT, Scorecard, then Six Sigma." *Australian Library Journal* 58, no. 1 (2009): 122–23; Julia M. Esparza, "A Librarian's Experience with Six Sigma Tools," *Journal of Hospital Librarianship* 8, no. 3 (2008): 332–43.

CONCLUSION

Reference librarians will flourish as library and information consultants, maintaining their competitive edge in the information age. This book demonstrates that librarians can easily assume the consultant role, because they already function as advisors. It introduces the tools and mindset required to sustain a successful consulting practice, and effectively build and maintain customer relationships. Using these tools, library and information consultants can quickly adapt services to shifting consumer expectations and the changing information environment.

Consultants, like librarians, sell advice, helping consumers to define their needs, develop the skills and competencies to address these needs, and take action. Drawing from the reservoir of knowledge they've acquired throughout their education and career, consultants seek to identify the root cause of a client's problem and develop a solution that will eliminate or resolve the client's problem. Businesses recognize consultants and consultants deliver results. Consultants attract business by consistently communicating the value of their services and results to the constituents they serve.

Librarians can better communicate their value to consumers using terms and concepts that are universally understood outside of the library community. Consumers choose to use a library's resources and services when working to resolve an information need, just as they choose the Internet, a bookstore, or other source of information. To remain competitive, library and information consultants must demonstrate their utility for helping the consumer to locate information both efficiently and effectively. This requires careful planning, along with a disciplined approach to proactively building and maintaining consumer relationships.

Since quality products sell themselves, the Voice of the Customer must anchor any library and information consultant's service product and marketing plan. Service products are especially difficult to design and implement, requiring consideration of many factors. The location and design of the service, employee skills and abilities, quality control, and the service's capacity and technological requirements all influence customers' satisfaction with the service product. The Voice of the Customer tools provide a mechanism for identifying and translating consumer requirements into the technical requirements necessary to satisfy their shifting expectations over time. The library and information consultant's goal is to design a quality product that either meets or exceeds consumers' performance expectations. This in turn encourages consumers to utilize the consultant's service repeatedly and recommend it to others.

While satisfied consumers effectively market the library and information consultant's services to others, establishing the consultant as a sophisticated brand is another effective means for communicating the consultant's value to current and future customers. Consumers rely on tangible evidence when formulating an opinion on the quality of their service experience. The consultant is better positioned to honor his brand's value proposition after maximizing the ServiceScape and detailing the processes and specifications to which a service must conform. Managing consumers' moments of truth regarding the service by knowing where service failures may occur and by proactively creating service recovery plans to address these failures also protects the brand's value proposition. Consumer opinions of a service are a function of all their previous moments of truth, making successful resolution of a poor service experience even more important.

A detailed marketing plan assists the library and information consultant with communicating the value of his brand, by forcing the consultant to identify and target markets for his service product, create a positioning strategy, and determine the appropriate mix of advertising and promotional activities. Quality marketing plans include measurable financial objectives or behavioral outcomes. This provides the consultant with the data to adjust the plan as needed and evaluate its overall success.

As stewards of the monies provided by a municipal, university, or grant-making organization, library and information consultants must allocate their financial, capital, and human resources in the most efficient and effective manner possible. This often requires that success be defined in terms of outcomes rather than profit. To satisfy customer expectations and perceptions, consultants must address gaps 3 and 4 of the Integrated Gaps Model of Service Quality by managing employee service roles and customer demand. The right individuals must be hired, empowered, and supported to successfully meet service designs and standards and deliver a service as promised. These individuals will serve as the face of the service product itself, and each must be capable of functioning as marketer, operations specialist, advisor, and sometimes leader, in an effort to address customer as well as library expectations. To minimize customer frustration and maximize library resources, demand for consultants' services must be managed with their supply. Special consideration of queuing models, the psychology of waiting, and techniques for smoothing customer demand when designing and implementing a service is also required.

Last, service quality functions as a product differentiator, influencing consumers' decision to use a library and information consultant's services or choose an alternative. Poor quality not only results in lost financial resources, but the waste of the lost customer. Once an established consumer is dissatisfied enough to seek an alternative, the organization must expend a considerable amount of time, energy, and resources to attract this individual back to their brand, or create a new passionate user of the brand's services. The disciplines of Lean, Six Sigma, and Baldrige National Quality Program offer organizations a systematic, deliberate approach for monitoring and continuously improving their products and services quality. While the library and information consultant may not work for a library organization with an established quality infrastructure, he can utilize the tools and philosophy driving these programs to strategically assess, monitor, and address the quality of his entire service portfolio.

Library and information consultants are positioned to help consumers understand the structure of information both within and outside of a library facility, to make sense of the information found, and to use this information in the format presented. By behaving and thinking of themselves as consultants, reference librarians can maintain their competitive edge, capturing consumers' attention in a crowded information environment.

INDEX

You may also be interested in

FUNDAMENTALS OF REFERENCE
Carolyn M. Mulac

The all-in-one "Reference reference" you've been waiting for, this invaluable book offers a concise introduction to reference sources and services for a variety of readers, from library staff members who are asked to work in the reference department to managers and others who wish to familiarize themselves with this important area of librarianship.

PRINT ISBN: 978-0-8389-1087-0
192 PAGES / 6" x 9"

MAKING SENSE OF BUSINESS REFERENCE
CELIA ROSS
ISBN: 978-0-8389-1084-9

WEB-BASED INSTRUCTION, 3E
SUSAN SHARPLESS SMITH
ISBN: 978-0-8389-1056-6

REFLECTIVE TEACHING, EFFECTIVE LEARNING
CHAR BOOTH
ISBN: 978-0-8389-1052-8

TEACHING INFORMATION LITERACY
JOANNA M. BURKHARDT AND MARY C. MACDONALD WITH ANDRÉE J. RATHEMACHER
ISBN: 978-0-8389-1053-5

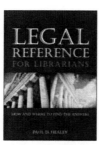

LEGAL REFERENCE FOR LIBRARIANS
PAUL D. HEALEY
ISBN: 978-0-8389-1117-4

THE WHOLE LIBRARY HANDBOOK 5
EDITED BY GEORGE M. EBERHART
ISBN: 978-0-8389-1090-0

Order today at **alastore.ala.org** or **866-746-7252!**
ALA Store purchases fund advocacy, awareness, and accreditation programs for library professionals worldwide.

CPSIA information can be obtained at www.ICGtesting.com
224955LV00003B/5/P